Effective Partnering for School Change

Improving Early Childhood Education in Urban Classrooms

JIE-QI CHEN   PATRICIA HORSCH

with

Karen DeMoss *and* Suzanne L. Wagner

FOREWORD BY BARBARA T. BOWMAN

Teachers College
Columbia University
New York and London

Published by Teachers College Press, 1234 Amsterdam Avenue, New York, NY 10027

Chapter 4 originally appeared as Jie-Qi Chen, Renee Salahuddin, Patricia Horsch, and Suzanne L. Wagner, "Turning Standardized Test Scores into a Tool for Improving Teaching and Learning: An Assessment-Based Approach," *Urban Education, 35* (September 2000): 356–384. Reprinted by permission of Corwin Press, Inc.

Chapter 6 originally appeared as Patricia Horsch, Jie-Qi Chen, and Suzanne L. Wagner, "The Responsive Classroom Approach: A Caring, Respectful School Environment as a Context for Development," *Education and Urban Society, 34* (May 2002): 365–383. Reprinted by permission of Corwin Press, Inc.

Library of Congress Cataloging-in-Publication Data

Chen, Jie-Qi.
 Effective partnering for school change : improving early childhood education in urban classrooms / Jie-Qi Chen, Patricia Horsch, with Karen DeMoss and Suzanne L. Wagner ; foreword by Barbara T. Bowman.
  p. cm. — (Early childhood education series)
 Includes bibliographical references and index.
 ISBN 0-8077-4414-X (cloth : alk. paper) — ISBN 0-8077-4413-1 (pbk. : alk. paper)
  1. Early childhood education—Illinois—Chicago. 2. Education, Urban—Illinois—Chicago. 3. School improvement programs—Illinois—Chicago. I. Horsch, Patricia. II. Title. III. Early childhood education series (Teachers College Press)

 LB1139.27.13C44 2003
 372.2 1'09773'11—dc22
                                                                    2003060098

ISBN 0-8077-4413-1 (paper)
ISBN 0-8077-4414-X (cloth)

Printed on acid-free paper

Manufactured in the United States of America

11 10 09 08 07 06 05 04   8 7 6 5 4 3 2 1

Contents

Foreword

IT IS A PLEASURE TO WRITE the foreword to this book. I was in on the beginning of the Schools Project at Erikson Institute, and even after I no longer worked on the project, I watched with interest its various twists and turns as staff adapted to each new challenge. I applaud the authors' desire to learn from the experience, but I am even more pleased that they are sharing their insights with the rest of us who daily seek to use our professional talents on behalf of teachers and children. Too often in schools, consultants come and go without taking the time to see if there are lessons to be learned.

My interest in the model of technical assistance outlined in this book began when I went to live in a small town in southern Iran in the mid-1950s. Typically, assistance to what were then called "underdeveloped countries" was simply another form of colonialism—Americans trying to impose their cultural systems and practices on others. Most often their efforts were either ignored or subverted. The project in Iran was to be different. My role was to help medical and nursing students understand the Western medical environment and consider how best to adapt it to local culture.

It did not take long before my idealism was overtaken by the realities of working cross-culturally. Many Iranian beliefs and behaviors conflicted with my deeply held convictions—convictions I had assumed were universal. It was only after I was able to accept that people really do have different beliefs, values, hopes, and fears that the search for how to be helpful began. I struggled to communicate what I knew to people who saw the world from a quite different perspective, and to accept that they would not always choose to solve problems my way.

My next experience as a consultant was in the early days of Head Start. In the mid-1960s, there were few preschool teachers and even fewer early educators who had experience working in low-income and minority communities. Inasmuch as I was experienced in both privileged and underprivileged White and African-American settings, I felt well qualified. It did not take long to realize that despite being "at home," the problems I was encountering were similar to those I had faced in Iran: I did not know the ins and outs of the various organizations and communities with which I was working, and most of them did not operate the way I thought they would or believed they should.

The potential for miscommunication was quickly apparent. Even the simplest interactions showed the chasm between my experience and that of the groups I was trying to help. Some of the lessons were small and amusing. I remember the confusion on the face of a teacher whom I admonished for allowing a little boy to spread paste all over his head and face. She said she thought his behavior rather odd, but, she explained, I had emphasized that children should be free to experiment and explore. Other miscommunications were more serious and uncomfortable. Teachers on an Indian reservation thought I was rude because I never waited for them to talk, while I thought them unresponsive because they didn't talk readily.

Not only was communication a problem, but my recommendations often did not work in programs I was assisting. Free play and an informal curriculum were energizing and intellectually challenging in one program, but caused management problems in another. After a number of years, I began to realize that to be helpful, consultants need to use their knowledge flexibly, within the context of the particular school or program. The principles may be the same, but how they are implemented is always different from one place to another.

Head Start's enabling approach, which Erikson Institute followed as the model for partnering during the Schools Project, grew out of a recognition of consultants' need to be responsive to a program's or school's context. I was one of six consultants who first implemented the enabling approach in the early 1970s, as part of Head Start's Planned Variation project, a national experiment designed to test the efficacy of various early childhood models. Predicated on collaboration and flexibility, the enabling approach, the six of us discovered, is complex, demanding, and time-consuming, but when it works, change is embedded in the school or program, rather than dependent upon the consultant.

This book is about enabling. It describes the experiences of a team of consultants working in nine public elementary schools in Chicago as they struggled to communicate the theories and strategies of developmentally appropriate practice to teachers and administrators. In the process, the Schools Project team had to cope with everything from systemwide reform mandates to racial and cultural conflicts, which forced them to redefine problems and find acceptable compromises. When they were successful, they were exuberant; when they failed, their feelings of futility and self-doubt were painful. Nevertheless, the enthusiasm this group retained for its work over the 11-year course of the Schools Project is heartening. This book is a testament to the belief that the principles of early childhood development and learning are universal, and it is our job to find out how to get the principles to work locally.

—Barbara T. Bowman

Acknowledgments

THIS BOOK IS A RECORD of and a reflection on the Schools Project, an 11-year partnership between Erikson Institute and nine Chicago public elementary schools, the goal of which was to improve the learning opportunities for young children in low-income urban neighborhoods through a variety of school-based interventions. The project was initiated with a grant from the W. K. Kellogg Foundation, which was subsequently joined by the Borg-Warner Foundation, the Joyce Foundation, the Polk Bros. Foundation, and the Chicago Annenberg Challenge. In addition, the W. K. Kellogg Foundation provided support for the writing of this book, for which we are very grateful. To have the opportunity to distill the lessons from 11 years of partnering was a real gift.

Many individuals and institutions participated in the work of the Schools Project. On Erikson's project team, we were joined by, in alphabetical order, Joan Berger, Elizabeth Beyer, Barbara Bowman, Jill Bradley, Gail Burnford, Christine Davis, Marie Donovan, Warren Dym, Deirdre Graziano, Renee Salahuddin, Julie Walstra, and Daria Zvetina. Some of these team members were regular project staff, while others served as consultants on specific aspects of the project. All were essential to the initiative.

Over the years of the project, we also received considerable advice and assistance from many colleagues at Erikson and elsewhere. We particularly want to thank David Beer, Marlynn Clayton, and Joan McLane. There were also quite a few Erikson students who spent their internships working on the Schools Project: Dorothy Carpenter, Susan Danby, Kathy Hofschield, Tammy Kerouac, Cynthia LeRoy, Dorothy Miller, Danielle Norman, Meredith Stubbs, Carol Stutzman, and Jennifer Wittenbrink.

In the Chicago Public Schools central office, the staff of the Department of Early Childhood Education, and in particular Velma Thomas, were extremely supportive of the Schools Project. We were also fortunate to work with Jean Borger and Carol Pearlman in the Department of Student Assessment.

In writing this book, we owe many thanks to Marie Donovan, who worked on early versions of chapter 3, and to Ruanda Garth McCullough, a co-author of chapter 9. Susan Liddicoat, our editor at Teachers College Press, provided valuable comments and thoughtful encouragement along the way, and Chris Simons at Erikson provided all kinds of behind-the-scenes support in preparing the manuscript. Aureliano Vázquez at Teachers College Press shepherded the book through the production process.

Of course, the Schools Project wouldn't have been possible without our nine partner schools—all of the teachers, students, administrators, and parents we worked alongside. As this book documents, university–school partnerships are not always easy, but the hard work of school reform created lasting relationships, and we still love to return to the project schools and follow their progress.

And finally, there is Barbara Bowman. We've already thanked her once in these acknowledgments, for her role as a Schools Project team member. In fact, she was a co-director of the project during its first two phases, and her wisdom and experience infused virtually every aspect of the project. But beyond the Schools Project, as a founder, former president, and still unbelievably active faculty member of Erikson Institute, she has inspired us through her unceasing efforts to improve early childhood programs, particularly for disadvantaged children, and through her willingness to continually question her assumptions about child development and learning.

Introduction

THE SCHOOLS PROJECT WAS an 11-year partnership between Erikson Institute and nine public elementary schools in Chicago. Initiated in 1987 with support from the W. K. Kellogg Foundation, the project sought to optimize learning opportunities for young urban children through a variety of school-based interventions. While there is much to learn from each of the interventions, many of which are described in this book, the Schools Project also provides important lessons on building university–school partnerships. For such initiatives, the partnership relationship is the crucible in which an intervention takes shape, and planning, implementation, and outcomes must all be viewed within its context.

Erikson Institute's approach to partnering for the Schools Project was reflective of its educational philosophy. Founded in Chicago in 1966, Erikson is a private graduate school and research center for advanced study in child development. At the Institute, learning among children is viewed from a social, relationship-based perspective that draws on the work of Jean Piaget, Lev Vygotsky, Barbara Rogoff, and others. From this perspective, children learn most deeply in and through relationships that allow them to manipulate, explore, and actively participate in a variety of activities (Bredekamp & Copple, 1997; Piaget, 1976). In particular, social interaction with adults and more competent peers through guided participation is an important vehicle for children's learning (Rogoff, 1990, 1998; Vygotsky, 1978, 1986). The child is not a vessel waiting to be filled with knowledge, but an active, engaged partner in the learning process.

Erikson Institute believes that relationships are key to the development of its own adult students as well. In its teacher education programs, Erikson fosters supportive relationships between faculty and students—and among the students themselves—through a variety of approaches, including one-on-one tutorials, small-group seminars, and lengthy internships and research projects that are attentively mentored. The goal of these relationships is to facilitate critical, reflective thinking among students that will lead to growth as individuals and teachers. Carefully nurtured, trusting relationships with faculty and peers provide an arena for risk-taking, as well as for learning to consider various perspectives, articulate disagreements, and appreciate differences.

Given this background, it's not surprising that in undertaking the Schools Project, Erikson would be concerned with the nature and quality of the partner relationships and would view those relationships as the catalyst for school change. The university–school relationship, of course, is not exactly analogous to the relationship between teachers and students. In particular, the university and the school come together as equals, each party with its own professionals who must find a way to draw on one another's knowledge and experience and work together on behalf of children.

For the Schools Project to be successful, Erikson believed that the university–school relationships would have to be "responsive": There would have to be a high degree of communication, trust, and mutuality between the partners, allowing for an ongoing process of dialogue and reflection—back and forth, and back and forth again, always growing and changing. The efforts to build and sustain responsive partnerships were as central to the Schools Project as any of the interventions implemented during those 11 years.

In writing this book, we have tried to represent both the university and school sides of the Schools Project experience. As co-directors of the Schools Project at Erikson Institute, our natural perspective is from the university side, drawing not only on our own experiences, but those of the 12 other team members as well (see Appendix A, Table A for brief descriptions of the team members). Conveying the perspective of the partner schools was more challenging, especially since schools—and even individuals within schools—had different experiences in the project. In describing their experiences, we have relied heavily on the third-party evaluation of the Schools Project conducted by researchers from the University of Chicago. In particular, throughout the book we have integrated quotations from teachers and administrators drawn from interviews, surveys, focus groups, and other components of the evaluation. The incorporation of their voices has resulted in a much richer and more complete account of the Schools Project, revealing the varied issues and competing agendas that shape university–school partnerships and can either help or hinder educational change.

THE PLAN OF THE BOOK

The book is divided into three parts: (1) the historical context and conceptual framework for the Schools Project; (2) a description of the major interventions implemented during the project; and (3) lessons from the project from the perspectives of both the partner schools and Erikson Institute.

Part I includes two chapters. Chapter 1 describes the school reform crisis in Chicago that led to the birth of the Schools Project in 1987. We chart the course of systemwide reform efforts during the project's 11-year history and discuss how they shaped the development of the project into three distinct phases. The chapter also includes profiles of the nine urban schools that were partners in the Schools Project, all of which serve primarily children from low-income families.

Chapter 2 describes the conceptual framework for partnering in the Schools Project. Erikson Institute adapted the enabling approach, which was developed by the national Head Start program in 1970 and resonated with Erikson's philosophy and experience. Several key assumptions underlie the enabling approach:

1. A preconceived educational program brought in from outside needs to be adapted to the circumstances of individual schools and teachers.
2. Teachers' engagement and support are more likely to occur when they play an active role in identifying needs and developing goals.
3. The quality of the relationship between a school and the "enabling" partner is directly related to the quality of school growth and change that occurs.

In chapter 2 we also describe the specific activities that characterized how project staff actually went about implementing the enabling approach in their day-to-day efforts to build responsive partnerships.

Each of the five chapters in part II is devoted to an area of intervention for the Schools Project. Chapter 3 discusses the Schools Project's activities in regard to curriculum and instruction. In general, these activities were grounded in the principles of developmentally appropriate practice. Outlined in the chapter, these principles—and the curricular and instructional approaches based on them—were completely new to many of the teachers in the partner schools. Skepticism about developmentally appropriate practice abounded, and progress was also slowed by teachers' need to deepen their knowledge in various subject areas and to build their repertoire of teaching methods. Efforts around curriculum and instruction went on over the entire course of the Schools Project, and as we worked with the partner schools to integrate developmentally appropriate practice, we found ourselves changing as well, as teachers' responses to our efforts forced us to reconsider some of our assumptions about developmentally appropriate practice, particularly in the context of schools serving at-risk children.

In chapter 4, the area of intervention is the positive, productive use of standardized test scores. In 1995, when the Schools Project was well under way, the city of Chicago implemented an academic accountability system for schools based solely on standardized test scores. Not surprisingly, many teachers and administrators began to focus almost exclusively on raising scores. While we felt that Chicago's accountability system was shortsighted, we realized the Schools Project had to address teachers' and administrators' concerns, so we developed an assessment process based on analysis of scores. The analyses were used to determine areas of instructional strength and weakness and to formulate customized interventions incorporating developmentally appropriate practices to improve student learning. With this assessment-based approach, we were able to address the need to raise test scores without letting schools fall into the trap of "teaching to the test."

The next two chapters describe two ways that the Schools Project set out to improve the overall classroom/school environment. For prekindergarten and kindergarten classrooms, as discussed in chapter 5, we guided the process for accreditation by the National Association for the Education of Young Children (NAEYC). The topic of chapter 6 is the Responsive Classroom, a social curriculum developed by the Northeast Foundation for Children that can be used at all elementary grade levels. Both these efforts reflected the partner schools' desire to provide a safe, caring environment that fosters all aspects of children's development—cognitive, emotional, social, and physical.

In chapter 7, we discuss the integration of computer technology in early childhood classrooms. Computer technology is playing an increasingly important role in curricular and instructional practices; however, complete and authentic technology integration is rare. This is particularly true in inner-city schools, where it is often hard enough just to purchase computer equipment, much less provide sufficient training for teachers. For the Schools Project, we focused not only on teacher training, but also on the development of site-based technology leadership and expertise, to increase the likelihood of ongoing, effective technology use in the partner schools.

Part III consists of two chapters that summarize the major lessons from the Schools Project for university–school partnerships. Chapter 8 describes the findings from the third-party evaluation of the project. The University of Chicago researchers focused on the five schools that were still partners in 1998, the final year of the project, though they also conducted some evaluation activities at two schools that had left earlier in the project, which gave them the opportunity to explore questions about the sustainability of change after a partnership ends.

In chapter 9, we build on the evaluation findings, as well as our own experiences, to delineate the contextual realities that shape university–school partnerships over time. These contextual realities—school system

supports and pressures, the school environment and culture, teacher individuality and diversity, and the resources and limits of the university—
determine not only how university–school partnerships begin, but also how
they proceed and, ultimately, end.

Together, these two final chapters offer experience-based guidance
from both the university and school perspectives on building and sustaining a relationship that can serve as a foundation for improved teaching and
learning.

PART I

The Historical Context and Conceptual Framework

CHAPTER 1

"The Worst School System in America"

School Reform in Chicago and the Roots of the Schools Project

THE CHICAGO PUBLIC SCHOOLS IN CRISIS

DURING A VISIT TO CHICAGO in the fall of 1987, U.S. Secretary of Education William Bennett declared the city's public schools to be the "worst in the nation" (Banas & Byers, 1987). The system had about a 50% high school graduation rate, and half of its high schools placed in the bottom 1% of U.S. schools on the ACT college entrance exam. Prompted by a strong traditional union, principals and teachers were more focused on protecting jobs, salaries, and benefits than on developing a vision of school improvement; in fact, a 19-day teachers' strike over contractual agreements took place just before Secretary Bennett's visit. Population shifts resulting from immigration and middle-class flight had left some city schools empty while others bulged at the seams, and many of the school buildings were literally falling apart, with holes in floors and ceilings, peeling paint, inadequate plumbing, and drafty windows and doors. Sadly, Secretary Bennett's statement was not an exaggeration.

Soon thereafter, in 1988, the state of Illinois passed the Chicago School Reform Act, which called for each school to establish a Local School Council (LSC) comprised of six elected parents, two elected community members, two appointed teachers, and the principal; this group was to be the primary administrative body for the school. Among their responsibilities, LSCs, rather than the school system's central administration, would have the authority to hire and fire principals and disburse discretionary state

Chapter 1 funds and federal Title I funds; principals, in turn, would have the authority to recruit and hire teachers. These moves represented huge changes for Chicago's schools: Suddenly, responsibility for many important hiring and budget decisions rested with the schools themselves rather than the district administration.

This shift to site-based management led to the innovative use of discretionary funds in many schools. Freed from the central bureaucracy, some schools began to purchase books and computers, institute longer school days, and hire more teacher aides and parent assistants. They also used discretionary funds to partner with universities, arts organizations, museums, school reform groups, and others in efforts to help teachers be more innovative and effective in the classroom.

Despite significant improvements in some schools, in most cases these activities did not result in the degree of change hoped for in the legislation (Chicago Board of Education, 1988; Designs for Change, 1982, 1985; Moore, 1990). In 1995, the state amended the School Reform Act to give the mayor of Chicago the authority to appoint city school board members and top administrators and to address school performance. While LSCs remained intact, the amended act created a new layer of centralization, and the mayor quickly appointed a school reform board, which he made responsible for negotiating teacher contracts, improving the deplorable physical condition of Chicago's schools, and developing an academic accountability system for the district.

The issue of academic accountability proved to be particularly controversial (Bryk, Thum, Easton, & Luppescu, 1998; Chen, Salahuddin, Horsch, & Wagner, 2000; Duffrin, 1998). The school reform board decided to shift the accountability focus from criteria such as teacher certification and hours of instructional experience to student performance on standardized tests; while standardized tests had long been administered in Chicago, never before had scores been used as the sole criterion to judge the overall quality of a school and its teachers. In many schools, this round of reform reversed the interest in pedagogical innovation that had been prompted by the 1988 reforms: Threatened with school probation and afraid of job loss, principals and teachers began to narrowly focus their energies on improving students' test scores. This tension between performing well on standardized tests and incorporating pedagogical best practices continues to this day in the Chicago school system and elsewhere around the country, as high-stakes testing has become the common measure of accountability (Bryk, Sebring, Kerbow, Rollow, & Easton, 1999; Neill, 1997; Olson, 1998; Vaughn, 1998; Wiggins, 1998).

NATIONAL REFORM MOVEMENTS

The reform crises in the Chicago Public Schools (CPS) did not occur in isolation, but at a time of national concern about the education and well-being of children. In 1983, the publication of *A Nation at Risk* galvanized school systems across the country (National Commission on Excellence in Education, 1983). Unfortunately, like many contemporaneous critiques of the nation's educational system, the analyses of the problems and the nature of the solutions did not take into consideration the rapidly growing body of knowledge about the development of young children (Association for Supervision and Curriculum Development, 1988; Early Childhood Education Commission, 1986; Katz, 1987; Moore, 1987; National Association of State Boards of Education, 1988). The authors lumped together all levels of education in their discussions and recommendations, without regard to the specific needs and abilities of children at different ages and their implications for teacher education and classroom practice. Moreover, out of concern for the nation's future economic strength, the authors advocated a "competitive" approach to education, including an increased use of standardized tests to assess and rank children and a focus on students' deficits rather than their strengths. Early childhood educators feared that such an approach would lead to children being labeled as failures at younger and younger ages.

In an effort to redirect and inform the reform movement, the National Association for the Education of Young Children (NAEYC) published a position statement on developmentally appropriate practices for children from birth through age eight (NAEYC, 1986). The statement outlined a set of principles for early childhood programs based on the most current knowledge about how young children develop and learn; in particular, it recommended the use of more active learning approaches based on a broader interpretation of young children's educational needs and abilities. While the NAEYC guidelines were a strong beginning, there remained many unanswered questions, especially in regard to issues of implementation.

In 1988, the Early Childhood Education Task Force of the National Association of State Boards of Education (NASBE) published a set of recommendations to answer some of the questions (NASBE, 1988). One important recommendation was that elementary schools establish "early childhood units" for children from four to eight years old. The central characteristics of early childhood units were a developmentally appropriate curriculum for each grade level, improved assessment, responsiveness to cultural and linguistic diversity, parental involvement, and training and support for staff and administrators. The task force envisioned a variety of models for early childhood units; the particular model implemented by a school would depend on the needs and resources of the community. Both the NAEYC and NASBE publications upped the ante for public schools around the country, and many embraced the challenge.

THE EVOLUTION OF THE SCHOOLS PROJECT

The Schools Project emerged out of this mix of national, state, and local reform movements. In 1987, with funding from the W. K. Kellogg Foundation, Erikson Institute entered into partnerships with four public elementary schools in Chicago. Initial funding was for 3 years, though the project ultimately lasted 11 with additional support from Kellogg, as well as the Borg-Warner Foundation, the Joyce Foundation, the Polk Bros. Foundation, and the Chicago Annenberg Challenge. Over the years, some schools left the project and others joined it, and the direction of the project changed as well in order to address the needs of partner schools as they sought to respond to state and local reform mandates, and also as the schools themselves changed. In retrospect, the Schools Project can be divided into three distinct phases.

Phase 1, 1987–91

The four original partnerships were part of the Adopt a School program established by the Chicago Public Schools in 1981. Through this program, community organizations, universities, businesses, and other institutions partnered with individual schools in order to provide much-needed resources and technical assistance. Different partnerships tended to have different purposes, and in the case of the Schools Project, the goal was to create early childhood units. The project began before the NASBE recommendations for early childhood units were published, but Erikson was already working with NASBE's Early Childhood Education Task Force and others on the development of the concept. With Chicago's Adopt a School program, Erikson realized it had an opportunity to try to implement early childhood units in whole-school settings.

During the first year, we collaborated with teachers in the partner schools to establish developmentally appropriate practices for prekindergarten classrooms. The collaboration extended to kindergarten classrooms in the second year and then to the first, second, and third grades in year three. By year four, all teachers from pre-kindergarten through third grade were participating in the project, though all five grade levels were not yet functioning as a cohesive early childhood unit in three of the four original partner schools.

Phase 2, 1991–95

For many teachers in the partner schools, the new approach to early childhood education raised issues around assessment: Traditional measures of student growth used by schools, such as the Iowa Tests of Basic Skills (ITBS), do not capture all the areas of concern in regard to developmentally appropriate practice, yet most teachers had no other methods for assessment. In response to this concern, the Schools Project shifted its focus to assessment of student learning, which marked the beginning of the second phase. We worked with teachers to devise performance-based assessments that would capture the full range of learning expectations for each grade level. By increasing teachers' expertise in various forms of assessment, we hoped to decrease their reliance on standardized testing as the measure of students' skills and knowledge. Additionally, teachers learned to use performance-based assessments to tailor curricula and instructional techniques to their students' needs.

Serendipitously, in 1993 the state turned its attention to student assessment, too, and developed a plan requiring the use of two assessment instruments. One of the instruments had to be a standardized achievement test such as the ITBS, while the other was to be performance-based. This state mandate provided additional momentum to the Schools Project's efforts during this phase.

While assessment and related curricular issues were the focus of phase 2, the Schools Project began to branch out during these years: Teachers in some of the partner schools also received training in reading programs, participated in discussions and workshops on multiculturalism, and began to incorporate computer technology in the classroom.

Phase 3, 1995–98

The third and final phase of the Schools Project was marked by the passage of Illinois's 1995 school reform legislation, which led to the CPS accountability system based on standardized test scores. Although meant to improve schools and student learning, the intense focus on test scores tended to inhibit the kinds of substantive reforms envisioned by the Schools Project. We found ourselves having to address principals' and teachers' redoubled focus on standardized tests, particularly in the three partner schools placed on probation for low reading scores. These schools needed to raise their scores and get off probation, and we wanted to help them do this, but without losing sight of broader educational goals. We continued to work with all the partner schools on developmentally appropriate curricula and instruction, though now we made explicit links between changes in classroom practice and improvements in test scores.

School accountability cast a long shadow during phase 3, but the Schools Project was involved in several other areas as well, ranging from the social-emotional development of children to computer technology. Despite the varied nature of the areas of intervention, they were all true to the Schools Project's overarching goal of improving the learning opportunities for young children in low-income urban schools.

During phase 3, Erikson Institute also contracted with external evaluators to assess the process and effects of the Schools Project. Ongoing internal evaluation had been integral to the project from the beginning: We regularly engaged in a variety of evaluation activities, such as teacher interviews and focus groups, classroom observations, individual teacher conferences, and surveys, in order to gauge the progress of the project and guide its continuing development. But an external evaluation was deemed important as well in order to gain objective insight.

The evaluation team, from the University of Chicago, was familiar with the Chicago Public Schools, as well as with the philosophy and goals of the Schools Project. The main evaluation took place during the first 6 months of 1998 and included the five partner schools that were still part of the project at that time. The team conducted individual interviews with teachers, curriculum coordinators, and administrators; distributed surveys; observed classrooms; and attended grade-level meetings and schoolwide events. They emphasized to the partner schools that it was an external evaluation and completely confidential. In the spring of 1999, the team conducted additional interviews at two partner schools that had left the Schools Project during an earlier phase, in part to explore the continuing effects of project interventions beyond the duration of the partnership.

The Schools Project ended in 1998, as the evaluation team was conducting its activities, with the exception of the project's NAEYC accreditation component, which continued until 2001. Among the schools still participating in 1998, we felt that most were ready to move beyond the project, either to other partnerships that would better meet their current needs, or to independence, made possible by the establishment of strong leadership and a cohesive professional community. Also, funding for the Schools Project ended in 1998, and while it would have been possible to apply for continuing support, Erikson Institute decided it was time to step back and reflect on the past 11 years. The writing of this book was a crucial part of this reflective process, an effort to distill lessons about the partnership process and project interventions that can be brought to bear on other initiatives, at Erikson Institute and elsewhere.

PROFILES OF THE PARTNER SCHOOLS

Over the course of the Schools Project, nine Chicago public elementary schools were involved, for varying lengths of time. (See Appendix B, Table B.1, which lists the schools according to the number of years of participation, from least to most; for this book, the names of the schools have been changed.) The four initial partner schools were assigned to the project by the Chicago Board of Education's early childhood department. The other five joined voluntarily at different times later in the project: Four joined because their principals became familiar with the project and wanted to participate; the fifth joined at the instigation of a small group of teachers who had met Schools Project staff at a local conference and subsequently encouraged their principal and Erikson to make the school a partner.

As indicated in Table B.1, in all nine schools the majority of students were from low-income families. African-American and Hispanic students were also highly represented, and in some schools they comprised the entire student body. In many of the schools, students' limited proficiency in English was an issue. High student mobility rates were also common among the partner schools.

As the profiles that follow show, however, the nine schools also differed in many ways from one another—for example, in terms of their neighborhood environments, their general attitudes toward reform and change, and even what they hoped to gain from participation in the Schools Project (Appendix B, Table B.2 lists the intervention areas and activities for each school). In addition, there were changes in most of the schools during their years of participation in the project, such as principal and teacher turnover, school renovations, and increases or decreases in the number of students. In any long-term project, these sorts of changes inevitably occur, and they affect the course of the project, sometimes making things easier, but other times harder.

For the profiles, the schools are described in the same order as in Tables B.1 and B.2: from least to most years of participation in the Schools Project. The longer a school was involved, the longer the profile tends to be, though none of the profiles attempts to be comprehensive in describing the school's history, culture, setting, or Schools Project experience. Instead, they are an attempt to convey the most salient features and issues—an overall image of each school—so that the reader has a general idea of the various environments in which the Schools Project operated.

Newley School/Stanton Child–Parent Center

Newley joined the Schools Project in 1989, 2 years into phase 1. The school's principal wanted the project to provide technical assistance to the brand-new Stanton Child–Parent Center, the preschool and primary division of Newley, located almost a mile away from the main building.

Stanton, bright and welcoming, draws its students from the surrounding neighborhood of recent Mexican immigrants. Most of the children, as well as their parents, are not proficient in English, so language development is a primary issue for the school. When the Schools Project began at Stanton, there were only a few teachers who spoke both English and Spanish and were also skilled in teaching basic literacy skills; the others spoke only English, had limited knowledge about teaching English as a second language, and usually employed traditional teaching methods. These circumstances made it difficult to support literacy development.

The Schools Project was asked to work with teachers to develop appropriate, effective literacy practices. Frequent conflicts between project staff and Stanton's administrators over teaching approaches and scheduling for professional development activities resulted in little change, however, and the partnership ended after 2 years.

Nathan School

Nathan is located in a neighborhood of brick bungalows and apartment buildings on Chicago's southwest side. The student population there increased by almost 40% between 1995 and 1998, its years of participation in the Schools Project. Until a new addition opened in 1998, it was extremely difficult to provide appropriate educational spaces for children. Before the addition, several classrooms were housed in the auditorium and library, and counseling and nursing services, as well as some administrative offices, were housed in converted rest rooms. Some students attended class at branch campuses: The pre-kindergarten and kindergarten classrooms met in a nearby Catholic school, while the primary classrooms were located at a local synagogue that was not within walking distance of the main campus. When the addition was completed, students in kindergarten through seventh grade all could attend classes at the main campus, though the pre-kindergarten classrooms remained at the Catholic school.

In the 1980s, as the student population began to increase, the ethnic and racial composition of Nathan also began to change: The school's substantial White and Hispanic populations almost disappeared and the once small African-American population climbed to more than 90% of the student body by 1998.

It was the principal's decision to join the Schools Project in 1995, and he made the decision without teacher input. His authoritative leadership style, which was evident throughout the course of the partnership, frustrated some teachers and caused them to be reluctant to engage in the project.

Teachers from pre-kindergarten through third grade were primarily involved in the project's activities, which included, among others, exploring developmentally appropriate approaches to teaching young children, implementing the Responsive Classroom approach, and participating in a school-based computer training class. The preschool teachers pursued NAEYC accreditation in addition to these activities. Also, some fourth- and fifth-grade teachers participated in the Responsive Classroom training along with the teachers from the lower grades.

Nathan was one of the five schools still participating in 1998, at the end of the Schools Project, so it was an integral part of the evaluation. Also, because the school's NAEYC accreditation process was not completed until 2001, we continued our involvement beyond the official end of the project.

Trujillo School

Trujillo's small two-story building is tucked away on a dead-end street among affluent high-rise buildings, close to a major public housing project on Chicago's near north side. The school serves students in pre-kindergarten through sixth grade; most of them are Mexican-American or Mexican immigrant children who are bused across the city from a southwest-side neighborhood where the school was housed until 1993, when its population grew so large that the board of education was forced to find another building for it. A small number of students—fewer than 10%—are African-American children who live either in the nearby housing project or on its fringes.

The "new" Trujillo on the near north side has a dual-language (Spanish and English) curriculum: In the preschool and early primary grades, all students are taught in Spanish for about 75% of the day, with the remaining classes taught in English; for older students, English is used about 75% of the day and Spanish is used the rest of the time.

The school has few ties to its new geographic community. For the parents and others from the home community who ride the bus with children each day and volunteer at the school, however, Trujillo is a true community of teachers and learners. Visitors are often struck by the number of parents serving as instructional aides in classrooms or pullout programs, and many teachers have created cross-grade tutoring programs so that younger children might work with their older siblings or other relatives who are students there. For the Hispanic students, Trujillo has a strong communal feeling and a family atmosphere.

The same cannot be said for the African-American students who attend the school. Its dual-language program, in particular, can be extremely frustrating for these students and their parents. Although the school has made efforts to address this issue, it has not yet been resolved.

Shortly before joining the Schools Project in 1995, Trujillo's principal brought together a team of teachers with a strong interest in dual-language and early education. Soon after the school joined the project, she became principal of another Chicago school, and approximately 39% of the teachers left each year over the next 3 years as leadership crises ensued (Duffrin, 1999). This high teacher turnover was a challenge for the Schools Project; yet, like Nathan, in a short time Trujillo got involved in a wide range of activities focused on the preschool, primary, and intermediate grades. While there was an emphasis on curricular and instructional issues related to the dual-language program, other areas of intervention included assessment, NAEYC accreditation, the Responsive Classroom approach, and computer technology.

In 1997, Chicago's school reform board told Trujillo that it no longer would be exempt from academic accountability based on standardized test scores, even though the tests used are in English, and the school was placed on probation for low scores. This turn of events shifted Trujillo's focus during the final year of the Schools Project, although the school did remain committed to NAEYC accreditation (which kept project staff involved into 2000). Trujillo was also part of the Schools Project's external evaluation.

Elston School

Located on Chicago's west side, Elston serves children in pre-kindergarten through sixth grade. Its completely African-American student body lives in the surrounding neighborhood of small brick homes and apartment buildings. The neighborhood's neat appearance belies the poverty and drug dealing that affect the lives of residents on a daily basis.

Elston was one of the four initial partner schools. Prior to joining the project, the school was involved in a reform effort to promote teacher decisionmaking and parent–teacher collaboration. This undertaking resulted in a strong sense of community among the teachers and in a vision of an Afrocentric curriculum that would enhance literacy skills and promote students' self-esteem.

Elston's principal hoped the Schools Project would help turn the Afrocentric curriculum into a reality, combining the history and culture of Africans and African Americans with innovative teaching practices in the areas of reading, writing, and mathematics. Also, during the 4 years that Elston was part of the Schools Project, teachers, parents, and project staff together created an African resource room, a publishing program for student writing, and a training program for grandparents to become classroom assistants. Elston's principal during the Schools Project was unwavering in her high expectations for faculty and students.

In 1991, when the first phase of the Schools Project ended, the partnership with Elston came to an end, too, because the school was not interested in performance-based assessment, the project's new focus. Individual teachers continued to be involved with Erikson Institute in different ways, however: For example, one teacher pursued a master's degree in child development at Erikson, while another teacher got her classroom involved in Erikson's arts integration project.

Ivy School

Ivy was one of the four initial project partners in 1987. The school is a large one, with pre-kindergarten through eighth-grade classrooms. When the Schools Project began, almost 1,000 students packed every available space; there were even four kindergarten classrooms in a partitioned school gym. Subsequently, an addition was built, but the student population continued to grow.

The neighborhood of single-family bungalows is ethnically diverse, with Asian, Hispanic, African-American, and White families. Among the children in immigrant families, limited English proficiency is often a problem.

Ivy has a history of strong leadership and traditional, skilled teachers who emphasize academic achievement. For the Schools Project, Ivy initially focused on curriculum and instruction in pre-kindergarten through third grade. At the suggestion of project staff, the school also eventually entered into a partnership with a suburban school to provide joint student activities and teacher workshops. This partnership was the catalyst for Ivy's envisioning an integrated arts curriculum that would include all the school's grade levels. In 1991, Ivy left the Schools Project and the next year began partnering with an arts-in-the-school organization in order to pursue this vision, although the school continued to focus on student learning in a child-centered environment.

In 1999, the Schools Project evaluators from the University of Chicago conducted follow-up interviews with staff at Ivy.

Nolan School

A group of teachers familiar with Erikson Institute and the Schools Project convinced Nolan's administration to join the project in 1991. Nolan was a high-functioning school that had already started to transform itself both physically and pedagogically when it joined the project. The LSC was led by parents and community members who had a strong vision for the school. The council set aside a significant amount of money for staff development, and teachers were encouraged to attend conferences and workshops and were paid a small stipend when they met together before or after school hours for planning and reflection. Prior to joining the Schools Project, teachers at the school had revised the kindergarten and first- and second-grade report cards and were learning about literature-based reading approaches.

The multiethnic and socioeconomically diverse student body at Nolan mirrors the northwest Chicago neighborhood in which it is located. During the early 1990s, when it was a new partner in the Schools Project, Nolan experienced changes in student demographics, like many other schools in the city at that time. The number of White children decreased and the number of Latino children increased; at the same time, the number of students from low-income families rose, as did the number with limited English proficiency.

Before Nolan joined the project, the school included pre-kindergarten through eighth grade, and overcrowding had become a serious issue. In 1990, a new middle school opened that the neighborhood's seventh- and eighth-graders began to attend, and though this helped a bit, space was still tight. Teachers agreed to let students eat lunch in their classrooms rather than the cafeteria, which was converted for other uses. An added benefit of this lunchtime arrangement was that the classrooms provided a more flexible and homelike setting for children's meals.

During its 7 years in the Schools Project, Nolan worked on curricula, instruction, and assessment; received NAEYC accreditation; implemented the Responsive Classroom approach; and tackled computer technology. The school was especially intent on involving parents. Among the many activities were a parent bookbinding program for student works, a regular family reading night, a computer training course for parents, and parent training sessions for the Responsive Classroom approach. Nolan School was also one of the sites that participated in the Schools Project's external evaluation.

Doyle School

Situated on Chicago's south side, Doyle serves children from pre-kindergarten through eighth grade. The student mobility rate tends to be quite high from year to year, the student population is 100% African American, and almost all the children are from low-income families. Most people in the community live in large brick multifamily dwellings, and vacant lots and empty buildings dot the landscape. The school serves as a neighborhood center where parents participate in adult education offerings and work as school aides.

Doyle joined the Schools Project in 1989 at the suggestion of its principal, a graduate of Erikson Institute who wanted to improve early childhood education at the school. At the time, Doyle was getting involved in a number of reform initiatives, taking a "soup to nuts" approach to staff development. In addition to the Schools Project, there were initiatives to integrate science and math curricula, develop a discussion-based literature program, and promote cooperative learning. Often it was difficult to coordinate all these initiatives, and the variety prevented the development of a coherent, systematic educational plan to support student learning.

In the early 1990s, Schools Project staff worked with Doyle faculty to develop an Afrocentric curriculum that gave students a chance to learn about and celebrate their identity and heritage. This initiative "took" more than the others, and there began to be noticeable changes in the classrooms.

In 1995, Doyle underwent a much-needed renovation: Buckling floors were repaired, new windows installed, and a cafeteria and multipurpose room built on. The next year, the school was put on probation for low test scores. Doyle remained in the Schools Project until its end in 1998, participating in a range of activities (see Table B.2), many of which were focused on improving test scores. The school also participated in the evaluation of the project.

Wheaton School

Like so many Chicago schools, Wheaton is located in a neighborhood that has changed dramatically over the years. Situated just west of the city's downtown business district, the community once was comprised of German, Polish, and Swedish immigrants; now it is mostly Latino (Puerto Rican, Mexican, and Central American) and African American. Multiunit frame and brick buildings line its long blocks, interspersed with recently built single-family public housing dwellings.

Wheaton's main building is a three-story monolith that extends the entire length and width of a large city block. During the Schools Project, the school enrolled almost 1,300 students in pre-kindergarten through eighth grade, almost all of whom were from families living below the poverty level.

An initial partner school in 1987, Wheaton asked the Schools Project to work with staff at the newly constructed child–parent center across the street from the main building. The preschool teachers there were very enthusiastic about the project and new approaches to early childhood education.

In 1990, the project spread to Wheaton's main building, as kindergarten and primary teachers there became interested in it. The initial enthusiasm did not last, though, because of the very different culture of the main building. While teachers at the child–parent center worked closely with each other and collaborated on their plans and activities, teachers in the main building operated as entrepreneurs. Any correspondence of curricula, instruction, or assessment from classroom to classroom was coincidental rather than planned. This culture was supported by the principal, who believed in teaching as an individual endeavor rather than a common enterprise.

In 1994, a new, more collaborative administration emerged upon the principal's retirement. This team asked us to assist the preschool and primary teachers in implementing a developmental approach to teaching and learning and to serve as in-house mentor teachers and ad hoc curriculum coordinators—roles we were performing informally already. We also worked with volunteer teacher leaders to explore and implement appropriate practices and to develop on-site staff development programs.

These efforts soon came to an abrupt halt when Wheaton was put on probation for low standardized test scores. In 1996, as the school began to work with the probation management team appointed by the board of education, it became clear that the school needed a different external partner for the probation process, and it withdrew from the Schools Project. The University of Chicago evaluators performed follow-up interviews at Wheaton in 1999.

Xavier South School

Xavier South, on Chicago's near south side, serves low-income African-American students in pre-kindergarten through fourth grade. The school is housed in two buildings: one for kindergarten on up, the other—erected in 1967 as a "temporary" structure—for pre-kindergarten classrooms. The front door of the main building is across the street from two public housing high-rises. Not infrequently, gunfire can be heard at the school, coming from the apartments.

The main school building is visionary in design, consisting of two three-story octagonal wings; each floor in each wing has five classrooms and a central open space. Before the Schools Project partnership, however, the teaching in these classrooms tended to be extremely traditional in both form and content.

Xavier South was the only partner school to be part of the project for all 11 years, which resulted in a wide range of interventions and activities (see Table B.2). The principal at the beginning of the project, trained in early childhood education, was eager to move beyond a traditional educational program. Many of the teachers, however, equated child-centered approaches with unstructured learning, and they believed their students needed a rigorous, structured classroom, so it was a difficult climate for the Schools Project.

In 1990, the school took an important step toward school improvement by creating the position of reading coordinator. Working closely with a project staff member, the teacher who filled the position began to provide on-site staff development in reading instruction; she also worked with children who were having difficulty reading. Eventually the position was expanded to include all subject areas, and the reading coordinator became the curriculum coordinator. Among her responsibilities was to conduct weekly grade-level meetings and, during the summer, weeklong grade-level assessment and planning workshops. The Schools Project played a critical role in supporting all of these activities.

In 1991, Xavier South got a new principal. His tenure was marked by a shift to strong teacher leadership within the school and the development of an Afrocentric curriculum. In 1993, Xavier South was recognized as an effective school by the Chicago Annenberg Challenge and Designs for Change. This public recognition opened the door for the school to participate in several initiatives in addition to the Schools Project, including one program to create a school website and another to provide training stipends for parents who assist in the classroom.

Needless to say, working with such diverse schools was a challenge for the Schools Project, as were the frequent changes in the schools. Fortunately, the partnership approach followed by Erikson Institute for the Schools Project, described in the next chapter, is one that is meant to accommodate and be responsive to these realities.

CHAPTER 2

The Enabling Approach

A Framework for Responsive Partnering

"WHO ARE YOU?" "Why are you here?" "Who sent you?" "Something must be wrong with my teaching if you're here." "Because of the teachers' strike, we're already so behind. How will I have time to do this project?" These were the types of questions and statements from teachers that greeted us at the beginning of each partnership. In every school, participation in the project was not decided consensually by school faculty but, in most cases, unilaterally by Chicago Public Schools administrators or the school principal. In one school, some teachers were involved in the decision to participate, but they were only a small group that did not represent the faculty as a whole. Erikson Institute was in the difficult position of partnering with schools where teachers—and sometimes even administrators—were often wary, defensive, or just simply overworked. Under these circumstances, how could the partnerships succeed? How could we create a genuine sense of common mission, of inquiry and collaboration—the key to successful school reform?

Over the years, working with community groups and educational institutions, Erikson Institute has often looked to the enabling approach, developed by the national Head Start program in 1970, as a framework for building productive, effective partnerships (Katz, 1971). The enabling approach is defined by three assumptions:

1. A preconceived educational program brought in from outside needs to be adapted to the circumstances of individual schools and teachers.
2. Teachers' engagement and support are more likely to occur when they play an active role in identifying needs and developing goals.
3. The quality of the relationship between a school and the "enabling"

partner is directly related to the quality of school growth and change that occurs.

The enabling approach bridges the extremes of the "expert consultant" and "school agenda" approaches, in which one partner dominates the partnership. The approach is individualized, collaborative, and relational, focused on the co-construction of knowledge and understanding through ongoing dialogue and reflection. Because of these qualities, it has much in common with Erikson Institute's general philosophy of teacher education (Stott & Bowman, 1996).

While the responsive dynamism of the enabling approach makes it attractive to Erikson, this same quality can make it hard to implement, and there were times during the Schools Project when the partnerships were less balanced than in an ideal world. In order to achieve a teacher's or school's goal, for example, we might be insistent about a particular intervention, based on our professional expertise. Or a school might be equally insistent, for example, in wanting to focus exclusively on standardized test scores in response to board of education mandates. It was a hard line to walk, and one partner or the other occasionally stepped over the line, but the enabling approach provided an ideal toward which to strive during the project and a framework for planning, implementing, and evaluating interventions.

Four areas of activity characterize the way we implemented the enabling approach: (1) building trusting, respectful relationships between partners; (2) helping teachers identify their needs and interests; (3) formulating individual goals through a process of mutual decisionmaking; and (4) developing plans for technical assistance and follow-up support. As illustrated in Figure 2.1, these areas of activity are recursive and often intertwined. Building relationships is an ongoing effort, as teachers and principals come and go, for example, and partnership goals can change over time, requiring shifts in technical assistance. With the enabling approach, the onus is on the "external" partner—in this case, Erikson Institute—to constantly assess both the process and outcomes in order to gauge the interplay among these four areas of activity.

BUILDING TRUSTING, RESPECTFUL RELATIONSHIPS

Many teachers and even some principals were initially distrustful of Schools Project staff. They knew that we would not be there unless some type of change was intended, and while change offers the opportunity for growth and progress, it also stirs fear because it challenges competence (Evans,

FIGURE 2.1. The Enabling Approach

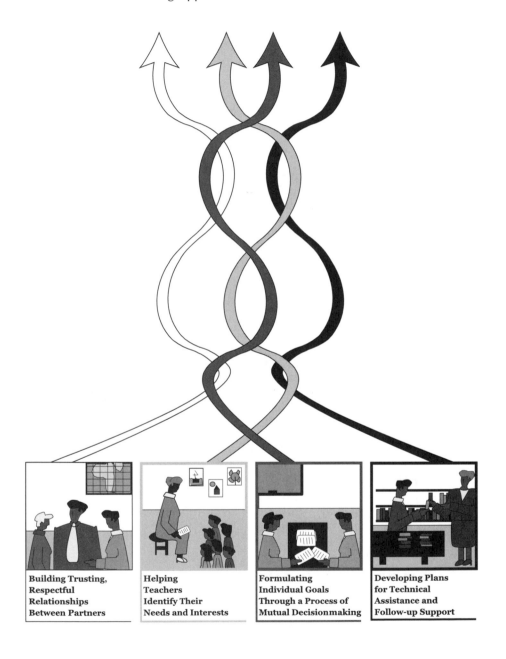

| Building Trusting, Respectful Relationships Between Partners | Helping Teachers Identify Their Needs and Interests | Formulating Individual Goals Through a Process of Mutual Decisionmaking | Developing Plans for Technical Assistance and Follow-up Support |

1993; Tyack & Cuban, 1995). Many teachers and administrators in the partner schools also had bad prior experiences with outside consultants or researchers who were dismissive, critical, and negative, and they worried we might be the same. For these reasons, our first effort in every school was to build trusting, respectful relationships. We hoped to allay fear and create an atmosphere conducive to questioning, self-reflection, risk-taking, and experimentation.

Trusting, respectful relationships take time to develop, however, and time is a limited commodity among public school teachers, whose daily schedules have little, if any, breathing room. We worked around this difficulty by adapting to teachers' schedules and attending some of their classes and meetings. In pre-kindergarten and kindergarten classrooms, for example, we took on the role of teacher's aide—reading stories to children or engaging them in other activities, cleaning up spills, wiping away tears, helping with bathroom chores. We were mindful that the goal was to develop a relationship with the teacher, not the children, and were careful not to usurp the teacher's authority in the classroom or let the children become overly attached to us. But by joining in classroom activities in this way, we were able to gain an authentic understanding of teachers in the context of their classrooms and, at the same time, reveal ourselves as real people and offer glimpses of our professional expertise. In most cases, teachers began to open up and share their hopes and concerns with us.

The task was more difficult in the primary grades. We started by sitting in on classroom lessons to get to know teachers and students. We watched and listened attentively and, if time was available afterward, asked questions or engaged in conversation with teachers about our observations in as unthreatening a manner as possible. Unfortunately, for the most part, the primary-grade teachers were unaccustomed to classroom visitors and became anxious and uncomfortable when we were present, so this relationship-building strategy was not as effective for them.

A more successful strategy was to schedule a faculty meeting to introduce new teaching techniques and materials. We offered book talks to introduce new children's literature to teachers, for example, showed videos on instructional strategies, gave presentations on different methods of assessment, and led workshops on integrating curricula. Often these gatherings led to further conversation with individual teachers, even requests to demonstrate a technique in the classroom, which provided the foundation for mutual respect and trust.

Another important strategy was to ask school administrators to allow teacher participation in the Schools Project to be voluntary. We believed that teachers forced to participate were likely to be disengaged or negative; by working only with those who were interested, we hoped to generate excitement (and good outcomes) that would draw in those who were initially reluctant. Teachers themselves echoed this opinion:

> I think first you have to ask teachers who are interested, and the ones that are not interested, don't get them involved that way. The teachers that are interested are the ones that I think will try to promote [the project] to the ones that are not interested at the time. I think that would be better, because you get a lot of negative feedback otherwise.

In some cases, principals did mandate that all teachers be involved with the Schools Project. Patty Horsch, a co-director of the project, remembers trying very hard to find some mutual interest or concern with a first-grade teacher required to participate. "Frankly," the teacher said, "I don't care what your program offers. I am not interested!" Knowing that the success of the project depended on good relationships with teachers, Patty gently persisted over the months, providing informational materials, encouraging her to participate in workshops, and inviting her to join visits to other schools. Eventually the teacher encountered strategies she wanted to incorporate in her classroom, and she became one of the strongest advocates for the project.

In a multiyear initiative like the Schools Project, relationship-building always remains a primary activity, not only because relationships need to be sustained over time, but also because new teachers and administrators get hired in schools and new staff join the project. Despite how time-consuming the relationship-building process can be, it is essential to the viability and vitality of the entire partnership.

HELPING TEACHERS IDENTIFY THEIR NEEDS AND INTERESTS

A key principle of the enabling approach is to actively involve teachers in the process of identifying needs and developing goals for themselves and their school. The paradox for Schools Project staff in using this approach was that for each partnership there was already a general goal established before we even set foot in the door. For the four initial partner schools, for example, the contract between the Chicago Public Schools and Erikson Institute was to create early childhood units, and that was also the expectation of the project's original funder, the W. K. Kellogg Foundation. Given these circumstances, wasn't a fundamental principle of the enabling approach already compromised?

The answer for us was no: The challenge was to achieve the preestablished goal in ways that would be appropriate for and meaningful to teachers. This could be accomplished only by inviting teachers to explore and articulate areas of potential growth, which also gave a sense of mutuality to the partnership and helped teachers begin to feel a sense of ownership for the project.

This facet of the enabling approach was sometimes unsettling for teachers. At the time the Schools Project began, in 1987, teachers in Chicago's public schools were neither encouraged nor empowered to push for educational change. Change was generally dictated from above—by the state, by the school system, or by the principal. This began to change somewhat in 1988, with the state reform legislation that called for the establishment of Local School Councils in Chicago, which were each to include two teachers. This legislation sent an encouraging message to teachers who were interested in improving teaching and learning, and some began to pursue professional development independently or sought out like-minded colleagues. Still, there remained many teachers who seemed content to continue as they always had in their classrooms, because they were either uncertain about how to change or simply uninterested.

In each partner school, we encountered both sorts of teachers. As relationships began to develop, some teachers naturally started to raise questions about children's development and educational practices, but often we had to intuit areas of concern or interest through attentive classroom observation and then initiate conversations with teachers. At first we tried to stimulate teacher inquiry by providing articles and materials describing new ideas and methods that addressed their concerns and interests. Many teachers found it difficult to imagine that these strategies would work in their classrooms, however; we realized the teachers needed to see classrooms where these ideas and practices were already in place, so we began to arrange visits to other schools.

Whenever possible, the visits were to schools that were demographically similar to those of the project teachers, to lessen the likelihood that differences between classrooms would be chalked up to differences between students. We always accompanied teachers on these visits and helped direct attention to salient aspects of the classroom setup and instructional strategies. After each school visit, project staff and teachers would meet together for discussion and reflection. Often teachers were overwhelmed by the differences between their classrooms and those they observed. The cognitive dissonance they experienced helped many of them begin to think about what they might like to do differently. We encouraged each teacher to identify at least one idea or practice from the visit that might be applicable to her own classroom. Frequently these discussions sparked enthusiasm and led to specific plans for teachers. For one partner school, a visit to a suburban school even led to collaboration between the schools' principals, a series of joint teacher workshops, and several holiday exchanges for students and their families.

In the external evaluation of the Schools Project, teachers identified classroom visits as one of the most valuable strategies for developing a vision of educational change:

> The Erikson lady took me and a few other teachers in my school to visit other classrooms. . . . We also talked to the teachers in that school. I was most impressed with how the reading was taught there. I must say that the Erikson lady had told me all of those strategies—word wall, read aloud, concept webbing, and probably many others—but until I saw another teacher doing those things in her classroom, I simply didn't believe that I could do it.

Another teacher said:

> Visiting the pre-kindergarten classrooms at Nathan School was instrumental to my mind-set for getting my own classroom accredited [by NAEYC]. I came out of their classrooms with a clear question: "If they can do it, why can't I?" And my answer was, "If they can do it, I should be able to do it, too."

FORMULATING INDIVIDUAL GOALS THROUGH A PROCESS OF MUTUAL DECISIONMAKING

Once teachers began to develop ideas about how their classrooms could be different, it was time to formulate individual goals. Following the principles of the enabling approach, this was accomplished through a process of mutual decisionmaking between teachers and project staff. At all times, an important role for us was to ensure that individual goals were in line with the general goal of the partnership, whether that might be creating early childhood units, or pursuing NAEYC accreditation, or integrating computer technology. At the same time, it was just as important for us to remember that for any of the partnership goals, there was usually more than one way to get there.

In partner schools where teacher participation was voluntary, the decisionmaking process was truly mutual and teachers were enthusiastic. The process moved forward through both formal and informal gatherings—regularly scheduled faculty meetings, in-service workshops, chance hallway conversations—and we played a variety of roles. In some instances, we found it most useful to act simply as scribes, taking notes as teachers brainstormed in a meeting, then distributing the notes for review and reflection. At other times, our role was more active: We would actually facilitate a meeting or ask questions to trigger teacher ideas. And sometimes we took the lead, presenting teachers with specific ideas to consider.

In schools where teachers were mandated to participate in the project, goal-setting was less mutual—and therefore less successful. In these cases, the principal often called a meeting that, for teachers, held more political than educational meaning. Many teachers offered little in the way of ideas during these meetings and would verbally assent to specific goals, then function in their classrooms as if no meeting had ever taken place. Also, in these meetings, differences among teachers could become barriers to goal-setting: Some teachers firmly believed in skills work as the foundation for primary education, others in constructivist approaches; some viewed teachers as authority figures in the classroom, others as collaborators with children; some preferred classroom autonomy, others considered teacher collaboration critical; some would never think of challenging administrative authority, others were more independent thinkers; some did not want to put extra time into the project unless they were paid for it, out of respect for their professionalism, while others felt that putting in extra time without pay was a sign of their dedication to teaching.

Some principals implicitly supported such resistance and friction, for while they required teachers to attend these meetings, they were reluctant to require them to implement changes in classroom practice. In these situations, we found it helpful to spend time with teachers individually, outside the group meetings, cultivating relationships and establishing an identity as something other than a monitoring arm of the administration.

As teachers set individual goals, we always encouraged them to choose ones that were realistic or to identify intermediate goals that would lead to achievement of a longer-term one. For example, Patty encouraged a teacher who wanted to create a more student-centered classroom first to move her collection of children's books from behind her desk to a classroom library accessible to the children. When the children gravitated to the books and demonstrated that they could use the library responsibly, Patty then suggested that the teacher create several learning centers. Those worked well, too. By this point the teacher was ready to explore new instructional strategies and began by trying a writing workshop. "Take the time and start small" was a constant reminder from project staff to teachers. Besides keeping teachers from getting frustrated and discouraged, this tactic had the advantage of being likely to result in classroom successes that would encourage other teachers to get involved in the project.

DEVELOPING PLANS FOR TECHNICAL ASSISTANCE
AND FOLLOW-UP SUPPORT

Once teachers had specific goals, it was possible to develop intervention plans, including the technical assistance and follow-up support to be provided by the Schools Project. Sometimes the intervention was a customized version of an established model; other times it was created from scratch. In every case, we took teacher expertise into account and built on what was already working in classrooms; we also made sure that intervention plans were in tune with the overall school culture.

While the Schools Project targeted early childhood classrooms (pre-kindergarten through third grade), most of the partner schools also had older students, and in several instances we ended up working with teachers in those classrooms as well. Many teachers of older students were interested in learning about computer technology, for example, or receiving training in how to foster students' social-emotional development. In these cases, we altered and expanded our technical assistance, in some schools hiring consultants with expertise on the educational needs and abilities of older children to strengthen the project.

No matter what the intervention plan, we always stayed involved to provide guidance and feedback and to adjust plans as necessary based on experience. This follow-up support was an important feature of the Schools Project. More often than not, teachers' professional development is not supported sufficiently in public schools (Horsch, 1992; Johnson, 1990; Sparks & Hirsh, 2000): Teachers attend workshops or conferences, but then are left on their own to gather materials and incorporate the new ideas and practices in their classrooms. In the Schools Project, as teachers implemented interventions, staff would meet individually with them and visit their classrooms. We would help teachers locate and organize materials with individual children in mind; we would be present when teachers introduced a new activity to children, to answer questions and solve unanticipated problems; we would accept invitations at the end of a unit or project to see students' accomplishments; and, perhaps most important, given how isolated teaching can be, we were always there to celebrate teachers' risk-taking and innovation. In many cases, the chance to share their growth with an interested adult motivated teachers to take another step.

While we never explicitly explained the enabling approach to partner schools, teachers instinctively understood and valued what we were trying to do:

> They are always there . . . to help if I have problems. I can always go to some of the other people from the Institute. And they're always willing

to help. . . . And, you know, they come in and try just to help us. It's never critical or anything. They don't try to criticize you or anything like that. And it's not "No, I wouldn't do that." Just show you another way of doing things. It's helpful.

Another teacher commented, "Marie was helping us with assessment and work on projects. We would run things by her and she would run things by us and we would work on [things] together."

In the third-party evaluation of the Schools Project, teachers characterized project staff as "not pushy," "about kids," "collaborative," "open," and "always there." Even the most lukewarm of teachers spoke of project staff not as "training" them, but "assist[ing them] in whatever problems or things that they would like to work on to enhance their teaching skills." One of the important aspects of the Schools Project is that it gave some of Chicago's public school teachers a chance to experience a different way of pursuing school reform: Through the enabling approach, many were able to see themselves for the first time as agents of change, true partners in the process of improving children's educational opportunities.

PART II

A Tapestry of Interventions

CHAPTER 3

Curriculum and Instruction

Opening the Door to Developmentally Appropriate Practice

IN 1987, ADMINISTRATORS IN THE CPS early childhood education department decided to try to improve the effectiveness of the city's early childhood programs by encouraging a comprehensive developmental approach to learning. At the time, most of the city's early childhood programs followed a traditional school-readiness approach, building curricula around discrete skills considered essential to future academic success and relying on highly structured, teacher-centered instructional techniques (Reynolds, Temple, Robertson, & Mann, 2001). In these programs, little attention was paid to the "whole child"; young children's social-emotional development, in particular, was overlooked (Fein & Rivkin, 1986). This tendency had intensified as the number of early childhood programs increased in the city's public schools: Because of a shortage of certified early childhood teachers, CPS had been forced to place many elementary and even middle school teachers in preschool classrooms; these teachers generally had a subject-area orientation and lacked knowledge of child development and early learning theory. In addition, the classroom assistants were usually community members, and though they provided valuable insights about and connections to the community, they generally had no background in early childhood education and were most comfortable in a teacher-directed, authoritarian environment.

As part of their efforts to develop strategies to promote program change, CPS administrators talked with Erikson Institute. Barbara Bowman, one of Erikson's founders and a faculty member, had been actively involved in development of the principles of developmentally appropriate practice (DAP), as outlined by NAEYC in its position statement on programs serving children from birth through age eight (NAEYC, 1986).

31

In this document, NAEYC identified two dimensions of developmental appropriateness: age appropriateness and individual appropriateness. Age appropriateness signified recognition of the predictable sequences of growth and change that occur during the first 8 years of life in the physical, emotional, social, and cognitive domains of development; knowledge of these sequences, NAEYC argued, should be used to create an effective learning environment for children at each age level. Individual appropriateness signified recognition of the variation among children in their patterns and timing of growth and change; sensitivity to this variation is essential to tailoring the learning environment to support the development of each child.

The NAEYC position statement also provided general guidelines, based on research, for developmentally appropriate practice in the areas of curriculum, adult–child interaction, relations between the home and early childhood program, and developmental evaluation of children. Several themes recurred in these guidelines:

- The importance of child-initiated, child-directed, teacher-supported play in the development of children in all domains, but particularly in the cognitive domain.
- The integrated nature of children's development, in that stimulation of one dimension of development affects other dimensions.
- The interactive nature of learning, whereby children acquire knowledge and skills "through active exploration and interaction with adults, other children, and materials" (Bredekamp, 1987, p. 3).
- The role of teachers and other adults as observant, responsive "scaffolders" in the learning process.

While the NAEYC guidelines were not detailed or even comprehensive, for the first time early childhood educators and caregivers had a document that set up clear distinctions between developmentally appropriate and inappropriate practices.

To introduce DAP to Chicago's early childhood programs, CPS and Erikson decided to create early childhood units in four elementary schools—the beginning of the Schools Project. The early childhood units would link five grade levels—pre-kindergarten to third grade—through a continuum of developmentally appropriate curricula and instruction, and the project was to pay special attention to promoting literacy skills.

The optimal intervention design would have been to begin with pre-K classrooms in the first year and add one grade level each year thereafter, so that by the end of 5 years the grade levels would be operating as a cohesive early childhood unit. The original Schools Project grant from the W. K. Kellogg Foundation was for only 3 years, however, so we decided that years three, four, and five would be compressed into one: that is, year one would still be devoted to pre-K teachers and year two to kindergarten teachers, but we would introduce DAP to the first-, second-, and third-grade teachers all in the same year.

As we embarked on the Schools Project, we brought with us two major assumptions about DAP. In regard to the students, we assumed— along with other proponents of DAP at the time—that as long as a classroom environment was age-appropriate, and as long as the teacher was attuned to differing levels of development in the class, all children in that environment, whether rich or poor, African-American or White, would make similarly rapid strides in their individual development. And in regard to the teachers, we assumed that introduction to DAP would encourage them to reflect on their current classroom practices and identify aspects of curriculum and instruction they could improve, making them eager for the types of technical assistance we could offer. These assumptions were challenged from the start.

STARTING OUT: PRE-KINDERGARTEN AND KINDERGARTEN CLASSROOMS

Encountering Uncertainty and Doubt

During years one and two, working first with pre-kindergarten teachers and then with those in kindergarten classrooms, we focused on two related areas of curriculum and instruction: the development of emergent literacy skills and the creation of a rich environment for learning through play. In both areas, many teachers were uncertain that DAP would help their students acquire the motivation and skills necessary to be readers and writers.

As we began to introduce DAP-based concepts and methods to support emergent literacy, such as reading aloud, story dictation, writing tables, and book corners, we discovered a fundamental difference between the teachers and ourselves in beliefs about how literacy develops and is promoted. We viewed literacy development as an emergent process beginning at the earliest age in the home environment, where children observe and participate in daily activities related to literacy, such as watching adults read newspapers, incorporating books and writing materials in play, and being read to. From these home experiences, children acquire a set of attitudes and skills related to written language (McLane & McNamee, 1990). Thus they start school with some notions as to what reading and writing are, a foundation on which teachers can build.

Most of the pre-K and kindergarten teachers felt that this scenario may be true for middle- or upper-class children, but not for the low-income, at-risk children in their classrooms, many of whom have few early literacy experiences at home. For these children, they argued, literacy development begins at school.

Many teachers also felt that child-centered, exploratory, play-oriented learning—central to DAP—was inappropriate for their students, who, they contended, need structure and direction to achieve school success. We were trying to expand teachers' view of classroom play as something more than just a respite from instruction. For young children, play is the primary mode by which they construct their understanding of the world (Jones & Reynolds, 1992). Thus we encouraged teachers to enrich their classroom space by creating learning centers with such things as sand and water tables, blocks, puzzles, materials for dramatic play and art projects, and other materials that afford children the opportunity to interact with one another, their teachers, and their environment. In particular, we encouraged a DAP-based, literacy-rich environment, including book corners where children can explore the books on their own, writing tables where they can practice their understanding of letters and sounds, tables with paper and pencils for scribbling, and literacy props to support dramatic play, such as books to read to dolls.

Many teachers were hesitant as they confronted these new ideas and wanted to continue using structured, teacher-directed instructional techniques. In regard to literacy development, for example, they favored a consistent, step-by-step process, beginning with telling children how to identify and form letters and asking recall questions about books. It was difficult for them to think of play as an opportunity to acquire or practice new skills:

> While I can understand this [DAP] works with middle-class White kids up north [in the city], my kids don't learn unless I tell them what it is they're learning. They don't know how to play to learn. They never get to play at home. They need us [teachers] to get them through the curriculum. There's no time for them to discover it. They don't know where to look. I'm Black and I know how I learned. This [DAP] isn't the best way, believe me.

Other teachers concurred with this opinion:

> The kids were kind of, I guess, wild. I mean, they needed a little more. I guess with the culture of our kids at home . . . if you knew the background of the home situation, you would understand that when they

come to school they do need more structure because they aren't exposed to it.

Like many parents in low-income neighborhoods, most of the project teachers believed that poor urban children, particularly minority children, learn best by being told (Goffin, 1988), and that they need more practice in conformance behaviors in teacher-directed group settings (Delpit, 1995; Goldenberg, 1994; Mallory & New, 1993). The changes we were asking the teachers to make did not correspond to their understanding of the role and responsibilities of a teacher, particularly in regard to preparing children for the expectations of primary teachers. Nor did DAP resonate with their knowledge of the children's home lives and parents' expectations.

Moving Toward Change

The strong reaction of the pre-K and kindergarten teachers forced us to question our assumptions about DAP. Perhaps most important, we realized that not only must curriculum and instruction be age-appropriate and individually appropriate, they must also be socioculturally appropriate. Particularly when there is a dramatic divergence between the home and school cultures, as was the case for many children in the project schools, any effort to improve curriculum and instruction must begin with an understanding of the life experiences of the children and their families, including parents' expectations of schooling (Bowman, Donovan, & Burns, 2000; Stremmel, 1997).

We were not alone in this realization about DAP. In the years following publication of NAEYC's 1986 position statement, an important criticism was that the conception of DAP was culturally and ethnically narrow (Bredekamp & Copple, 1997; Delpit, 1995; Garcia-Coll & Magnuson, 2000; Hart & Risley, 1995; Mallory & New, 1993). Since then, the field's understanding of DAP has become more sophisticated, accounting for sociocultural diversity, and NAEYC's 1996 updating of its position statement asserts that developmentally appropriate practice derives from three kinds of knowledge: knowledge of the stages of child development and learning; knowledge of the strengths, interests, and needs of each individual child; and knowledge of the social and cultural contexts in which children live (NAEYC, 1996).

Back in the late 1980s, however, as we worked with the pre-K and kindergarten teachers, we didn't have the benefit of the more sophisticated conception of DAP that evolved over time, so we had to work things out pretty much for ourselves, figuring out what DAP meant in different sociocultural contexts. The teachers were right—their students did need explicit instruction focused on letter identification, phonemic awareness, and other early literacy skills—yet we were right, too, in believing that the children could benefit from play-oriented activities that would develop and exercise those skills (McLane & McNamee, 1990). We began to think of DAP—and encouraged teachers to think of it—not as a set of prescribed best practices, but as an organizational framework that incorporates multiple ways of teaching and learning. It didn't have to be all direct instruction or all spontaneous play. It could be both. The key was to use the right approach for the right task at the right time, by being attuned to children's developmental strengths and needs (Barnett, 1995, 1998; Bredekamp & Copple, 1997).

As our understanding of DAP changed, so did teachers' response to it. Over time, and with considerable discussion and reflection with teachers, some real changes began to emerge. Classroom spaces were reorganized to accommodate learning centers and promote more varied interactions between teachers and students, including small-group and one-on-one interactions. Teachers began to make connections between home and school by introducing culturally relevant literature and building on children's rich cultural heritage. New learning strategies began to be incorporated into the school day, such as open-ended discussions and story dictations. In particular, we recommended that teachers experiment with children's dramatization of familiar stories, and we modeled the strategy. As we explained to teachers, this literacy activity has a definite structure, yet it encourages children to be active participants, using words from the text and re-creating the narrative (Paley, 1981).

Through these and other changes based on DAP, teachers began to see that learning basic skills could be more joyful and engaging for young children:

> I do teach the alphabet, words, nursery rhymes, and counting through whole-group work in the morning, but I also get children to play with these skills through games. I hide words in the classroom and let children search for them. We do counting games. I don't care if this is DAP or not, I know I am doing good.

Another teacher said:

> Well, they [project staff] just keep impressing upon us that you don't have to have such structure to achieve. . . . When you have been in a system a long time and all you've known is structure, it was hard because you just couldn't see how you could bridge that gap between

structure and nonstructure. With the little time that you do have, you got to try to get them where they are supposed to be. As a whole, I guess it took us a long time. I think we've gotten it.

The first 2 years of the Schools Project had been a big challenge, but our collaboration with the pre-K and kindergarten teachers was beginning to be fruitful. Now it was time for us to begin work with the primary grades.

MOVING UP: THE PRIMARY GRADES

In year three, as we moved up to the first, second, and third grades, we realized a flaw with our intervention design. We had assumed that when we moved up to the primary grades, the cohort of kindergartners who had experienced DAP would move up with us: Not only would the children be accustomed to a more student-centered learning environment, we hypothesized, but the effects of DAP would be evident in their emerging literacy skills, their ability to work together, and their desire to learn. These results would motivate the primary-grade teachers to learn about and implement DAP themselves.

Unfortunately, we'd failed to take into consideration the high rate of student mobility common to many low-income urban schools. During the Schools Project, the annual student mobility rate among the partner schools averaged almost 40%. This meant that there was not a critical mass of DAP-experienced kindergartners moving up to first grade in the partner schools.

Further altering our plans, many primary teachers had greater difficulty envisioning a DAP-based classroom than had the pre-K and kindergarten teachers. In the more structured and academic environment of the first, second, and third grades, most teachers were even more inclined toward direct instructional methods and preferred a whole-group teaching style. Our concern with this approach was that it did not address differences in children's skill levels and learning approaches, and it usually entailed a strict division between subject areas, reflecting district learning objectives. Moreover, the primary classrooms often lacked the materials—and even the space—needed to implement DAP.

Despite these challenges, there were areas where we felt we could build DAP inroads. Foremost, we decided to help teachers respond to a district mandate by working with them to align their curriculum with state and local learning standards, thus building a coherent framework for teaching. In the process of designing and implementing the new curriculum, we planned to introduce DAP principles and practices.

Organizing and Augmenting Curricula

Just prior to our moving up to the primary classrooms, CPS discontinued the use of quarterly criterion-referenced tests in all subject areas, which had been used to assess student progress toward achieving mandated learning objectives. These tests had provided teachers with focus and direction as to the knowledge and skills students needed to master each quarter and had served as a de facto curriculum. Their elimination left many teachers, especially those new to the system, without a clear set of expectations. Although CPS issued curriculum guidelines, they consisted simply of lists of discrete skills and facts to be learned, many of which were not age-appropriate or culturally relevant for students. Moreover, CPS did not provide any suggestions for activities, texts, or other resources to support instruction. Many teachers found the guidelines sketchy, confusing, and difficult to transform into lesson plans that matched available books and other classroom materials. One new third-grade teacher sought out Patty Horsch in her Erikson office. "What do I teach?" she asked. Even a veteran teacher said, "We were just trying to figure out what our goals were . . . and what topics we wanted to cover."

Working with the primary teachers, Patty, alongside Marie Donovan, Renee Salahuddin, and Elizabeth Beyer, created a curriculum organizer. Built around both Illinois's learning goals and CPS' curriculum standards for kindergarten through third grade, the organizer was divided into the subject areas of language arts and literacy, mathematics, science, and social studies. In each subject area, we linked skills and content knowledge to specific state and local learning outcomes at each grade level, with grade levels distinguished by color-coding. "The whole coordinating of the state goals with the goals of the board of education and our schoolwide goals was good," commented one teacher. "I think coordinating all of that was really a big help to us." The organizer also included performance-based assessment activities and rubrics, so that assessment of children's learning could be linked to curriculum planning—a practice advocated by NAEYC in its position statement on DAP (Bredekamp, 1987).

As Schools Project staff, we felt a bit like traveling salesmen, going from school to school with our materials to conduct workshops and also work with teachers at grade-level meetings and on an individual basis, so that they would understand the rationale for the curriculum organizer and how to use it to plan their lessons. Taking the state and local learning standards as a starting point, we helped teachers create an integrated curriculum—a DAP-based approach that links subject areas and helps students see the conceptual relationships among them. We also helped teachers create activities that would allow children to use their reading, writing, and other skills in authentic ways as they investigated curricular topics, in order to promote a deeper, more meaningful understanding of key concepts across subject areas.

For second-graders, for example, the mandated curriculum topic for social studies was communities, while for science they were supposed to learn about the life cycle and environment of various plants and animals. Linking the themes of community and environment, we guided teachers in creating a long-term project that started with the children studying their own school as a community and environment, then Native American and Pilgrim communities and environments, and finally the ecosystems of rain forests and deserts, including the plant and animal communities that are found in them. These spiraling investigations allowed the children to develop their understanding of key concepts related to the themes of community and environment, starting with their own school and then moving out in time and place. The thematic units also allowed for diverse activities across subject areas, from science experiments to research and writing assignments to art and music projects, so that children could develop a broad range of skills and knowledge. These qualities of the curriculum project imparted both coherence and depth to the children's learning, without ignoring state and local learning standards. There could be nothing more rewarding than when a second-grader announced one morning, "I get it! The desert is the opposite of the rain forest. One has no water and the other has plenty." A moment of conceptual understanding had occurred.

By encouraging all the teachers to use the curriculum organizer for planning, we intended to promote teacher collaboration as well as curricular coherence at each grade level and, within the primary grades as a whole, a spiraling curriculum.

In working on curriculum with the primary grades, the importance of sociocultural context to DAP once again became apparent. In some of the partner schools, this led to the development of either a bilingual or Afrocentric curriculum, often at the request of the school. It was actually work around one Afrocentric curriculum, however, that illustrates how concerns about the outcomes of DAP can sometimes cause a school to stick with a more traditional approach.

At Xavier South, which had a predominantly African-American student body, we worked with several teachers to create a DAP-based curriculum for African American History Month. Traditionally during that month, Xavier South second-graders, for example, learned to identify the names and contributions of famous African-American inventors, primarily through reading biographies and responding to questions about them. While these lessons expanded children's knowledge of cultural heroes, they failed to promote real understanding of the people and the context for their accomplishments. Children's journals might say nothing more than "He invented the stop light and he is a nice man" or "I like him, he is nice."

We sought to make more meaningful connections between the children and cultural heroes and to help the children recognize the personal motivation and effort inherent in their contributions. Thus, we recommended that kindergartners study several African-American illustrators of children's books and then illustrate their own picture books, so that they could see themselves as African-American artists. In a similar vein, first-graders would study African-American children's writers and then write and publish their own manuscripts; second-graders would study inventors and then create their own "patented inventions"; third-graders would study jazz and blues and then become musicians themselves; and finally, fourth-graders would study African-American leaders and then apply the qualities of positive leadership to their own role as the oldest students in the school. We also planned for every grade level to have relevant field trips and visitors, as well as exhibits and performances of student work.

Unfortunately, the school did not end up implementing the curriculum. Xavier South administrators expressed concerns about the time teachers would need to develop activities for the thematic units, as well as concerns about not having adequate materials for them. They also felt there was a lack of clear, testable outcomes in the units. Most of all, however, it seemed we had failed to convince Xavier South administrators that the methods of teaching and learning we were recommending would result in children's "knowing significant players in African-American history" and developing pride in their culture.

In the end, the administrators decided to make the study of African-American inventors a whole-school theme, with each grade level investigating the accomplishments of a particular individual. The instructional techniques were essentially as traditional as they had always been during African American History Month. Moreover, some of the inventors were not age-appropriate for the grade level. First-graders studied Charles Drew, for example, a pioneer in processing and storing blood plasma. Because the first-graders were just beginning to understand the concept of body systems, however, Dr. Drew's work held little meaning for them.

Increasing Teachers' Content and Instructional Knowledge

As the primary teachers began to use the curriculum organizer as a tool to coordinate their classroom studies, we noticed that many of them struggled because of limited content and instructional knowledge. For years they had relied on basal textbooks and scripted teacher manuals, so they had shallow, fragmented knowledge in subject areas and a narrow repertoire of teaching strategies. These constraints made it very difficult to implement a DAP-based curriculum. One teacher wrote in a note to Marie Donovan, "I can't believe I don't even know as much as what first-graders in the suburbs learn. Isn't this pathetic? How did the board ever let me through? What can I do? . . . I know I'm not the only one who feels like this."

To address the concerns of teachers, we offered a range of workshops and courses in various subject areas, including math, social studies, and reading. Some were taught by project staff, others by invited experts in particular curricular areas. All the workshops and courses were designed to link closely to the CPS curriculum guidelines and the project's curriculum organizer. Whenever possible, we scheduled follow-up sessions for classroom demonstration and observation, as well as individual conferences with teachers to provide feedback and help plan lessons and activities.

In the area of reading, for example, Marie Donovan and Renee Salahuddin taught a 6-week course totaling 24 hours for teachers in kindergarten through grade three from several project schools. We also hired a consultant to work with intermediate- and upper-grade teachers in the schools. Taking what is referred to as a balanced approach to reading (Weaver, 1998), they introduced teachers to a set of four interrelated processes for literacy development: word analysis (phonemic awareness, phonics), word identification (building a sense of sound and spelling patterns), word recognition (word meaning), and understanding connected texts (sentences, paragraphs). As part of the course, they also helped teachers devise developmentally appropriate activities to promote children's literacy development in each of the four areas and followed up with teachers in their own classrooms. One teacher explained:

> [Renee] came to my classroom, showed me how to do the story web to help my students better understand the text they were reading and also write better. She watched me do the same things. We then sat down to talk about how I did. She was very positive, saying that I was good. But she also reminded me of something I forgot to do. I find this way of learning is extremely useful.

Refining the Concept of DAP

Just as when we were working with the pre-K and kindergarten teachers, working with the primary teachers forced us to refine our ideas about developmentally appropriate practice. During years one and two of the project, we had realized that for teachers to be DAP educators, they need knowledge not only of the developmental stages in different domains and developmental variation among individuals, but also knowledge of children's sociocultural context. With the primary teachers, we realized that knowledge in these three areas must be accompanied by a deep and wide understanding of subject matter within and across disciplines, as well as a broad repertoire of teaching strategies. Implementing a DAP-based curriculum requires deep reserves of content knowledge and instructional techniques to draw on, particularly since teachers need to individualize curricular activities to meet the developmental needs of a wide variety of children. Many teachers need additional training to build these reserves, and in all the partner schools during the Schools Project, we spent considerable time on this type of professional development.

CONTINUING CHALLENGES TO DAP

Through these efforts around curriculum and instruction, everyone involved in the Schools Project began to change. For our part, as project staff, we rethought our assumptions about developmentally appropriate practice, particularly in the context of low-income urban schools, though we did not lose our basic faith in the importance and usefulness of DAP for all children. Many of our conceptual and practical adaptations, we would later discover, were being mirrored by other scholars and practitioners around the country, leading eventually to a more sophisticated understanding of developmentally appropriate practice in the field (Dickinson, 2002; NAEYC, 1996).

For the project teachers' part, most had begun to incorporate aspects of DAP in the daily routine of their classrooms, though only at one school—Nolan—were the first five grade levels beginning to function as a cohesive early childhood unit. Besides the challenges presented by many teachers' initial skepticism toward DAP, as well as their need to deepen their subject area knowledge and build their repertoire of teaching methods, progress had been slowed by limited administrative support in some schools; a lack of financial resources in the schools to support DAP-related classroom changes such as smaller class sizes, assistant teachers, and the purchase of books and other materials; and limited time in teachers' schedules for professional development activities.

With additional funding obtained by Erikson Institute, we were able to extend the Schools Project. As we continued to try to improve curriculum and instruction in the project schools, we ran into the biggest challenge of all in regard to DAP, high-stakes testing, a challenge tackled in the next chapter.

CHAPTER 4

Standardized Tests

Turning Students' Scores into a Tool for Improving Skills

THE CHICAGO PUBLIC SCHOOLS has administered the Iowa Tests of Basic Skills (ITBS) since 1975. Initially, administrators used the test to learn how well Chicago students were performing compared to national norms, and attention to the scores was minimal (Bryk, Thum, Easton, & Luppescu, 1998). In 1996, the scene changed. As part of its reform efforts, the Chicago Board of Education began to use the ITBS as the indicator of elementary schools' academic performance, and schools where fewer than 15% of students scored at or above national norms on the reading section of the test were put on academic probation. In virtually every school in the district, the new emphasis on standardized test scores quickly became a powerful force shaping administrators' and teachers' decisions and behavior at work.

The first year of the new accountability policy, 15% (71) of Chicago's elementary schools were placed on probation. Two of these schools—Doyle and Wheaton—were Schools Project partners; the percentage of students performing at or above national norms for reading was 13.8 and 13.5, respectively. Like all other schools on probation, they were required to work closely with a team that included a probation manager assigned by the school district, a representative from the district's Office of Accountability, and an external partner chosen to assist with improving reading scores. Schools on probation received considerable support to raise scores, but teachers and administrators were acutely aware that if scores didn't improve, the central administration had the power to fire them or even close down the school entirely.

For Wheaton, being on probation resulted in the end of participation in the Schools Project. Up to that point, we had worked only with the school's preschool and primary grades, and Wheaton administrators wor-

43

ried about our ability to work with the upper-level classrooms during the probation process. While we felt we could bring on a team member with the expertise to work with the upper-level grades, we were worried about the size of the school—about 1,300 students: We weren't sure we could develop the capacity to work with so many classrooms. After some discussion, there was a mutual decision that Wheaton should seek another external partner for the probation team.

For Doyle, probation served to strengthen the relationship with the Schools Project. Doyle had been a project partner since 1989, and almost every year thereafter the school's ITBS reading and math scores had improved, albeit in small increments. Believing that the Schools Project had played a role in these gains, Doyle asked us to be the external partner on the probation management team, to help improve the reading program. The teachers already viewed us as effective agents of change, both sensitive to the school's realities and committed to its success, and from then on we stepped up our involvement at Doyle in an effort to help the school get off probation.

One of the first things we did was to form a project probation team consisting of four project staff members: Renee Salahuddin, Patty Horsch, Jie-Qi Chen, and Marie Donovan. Renee had been the primary staff member at Doyle for 4 years, and her deep understanding of the school's culture and long-standing relationships with teachers, children, and parents in the school made her the ideal leader for our probation team. The other three team members, who also had ongoing responsibilities at other project schools, each played a specific role on the team based on their strengths: Patty closely monitored the overall probation process and helped negotiate with school administrators and the district probation manager; Jie-Qi spearheaded analyses of test score data; and Marie served as the early literacy expert. In addition, we contracted with a reading specialist to assist the intermediate- and upper-level grades.

Despite the school's vote of confidence, the project probation team struggled with the question of how to address teachers' and administrators' focus on improving test scores without sacrificing educational best practice. It was true then as now that a focus on test scores can result in teaching that mirrors the form and content of the test, thereby distorting and narrowing curricula and instructional methods (Haney, 2000; Heubert & Hauser, 1999; Klein, Hamilton, McCaffrey, & Stecher, 2000). The team wanted to ensure that Doyle did not fall into the trap of "teaching to the test" in an effort to get off probation.

On the other hand, it was clear that if Doyle's teachers and administrators were to stay the course with the Schools Project, the team had to acknowledge the new importance of test scores to the school community and explicitly integrate them into the ongoing process of improving curriculum and instruction. Despite their belief that standardized test scores should never be the sole criterion for judging schools, teachers, or students, the team members did not debate the wisdom of accountability systems based on standardized test scores nor question the validity of those scores, since the district's accountability system was unlikely to disappear anytime soon. With all the limitations of standardized tests in mind, they sought to use the scores toward positive ends—namely, as an assessment instrument and as a means to engage the faculty in efforts to improve teaching and learning at Doyle.

MAKING CONNECTIONS BETWEEN TEST SCORES AND CLASSROOM PRACTICES

When Doyle teachers learned their school was on probation, they were panicky, confused, and angry. Many attributed the low reading scores to the problems of students and their families, which they felt powerless to change. The children were "unprepared" and "unmotivated," teachers said; parents weren't supporting what they were doing in school; and families' frequent moves prevented educational continuity and stability. In response to teachers' concerns, Jie-Qi decided to use analyses of ITBS scores to explore student mobility, motivation, and preparedness, to see whether these factors were contributing to the low reading scores.

Student Mobility

Doyle did have a high student mobility rate: During the course of the Schools Project partnership, the average annual rate was 51%. But was this affecting test scores? In the field of education, many researchers have examined the relationship between student mobility and achievement, and the findings have varied: Some studies concluded that mobility had no significant negative impact on the performance of transient students; some indicated that mobility resulted in low performance; and others found that mobile students actually performed better than stable students (see Heywood, Thomas, & White, 1997, for a description of these different studies).

Given Doyle's high mobility rate, the probation team deemed it important to examine what kind of effect, if any, it was having on students' reading scores. Jie-Qi first compared the ITBS reading scores of students defined as either stable or mobile within a single academic year. "Stable" students were those who enrolled at Doyle before October 1 and stayed there at least until they took the ITBS in May. "Mobile" students were those who transferred to Doyle on or after October 1 and took the ITBS there in May. The analysis showed no statistically significant differences between the grade-equivalent gains for the two types of students in any of the grades at Doyle (see Table 4.1).

Considering that the effects of mobility might be cumulative, Jie-Qi next analyzed the reading scores of Doyle's fifth-graders to examine the impact of multiyear transience on performance. She compared the scores of those fifth-grade students who had attended Doyle for at least 3 consecutive years (fall 1993 to spring 1996) to the scores of those who had at-

TABLE **4.1.** The Effects of Within-Year Mobility on ITBS Reading Scores

Grade and Group	Average Grade-Equivalent Gain in Reading Scores (1.0 is a gain of 1 year in reading achievement)	Difference in Grade-Equivalent Gains
Second grade		
Mobile students	0.21	−0.21
Stable students	0.42	
Third grade		
Mobile students	0.82	0.29
Stable students	0.53	
Fourth grade		
Mobile students	1.18	0.26
Stable students	0.92	
Fifth grade		
Mobile students	1.06	0.23
Stable students	0.83	
Sixth grade		
Mobile students	1.51	0.50
Stable students	1.01	
Seventh grade		
Mobile students	1.06	−0.34
Stable students	1.40	
Eighth grade		
Mobile students	1.29	0.01
Stable students	1.28	

Source: ITBS reading scores provided by the Chicago Board of Education.

Note: None of the differences in grade-equivalent gains were found to be statistically significant.

tended two or more schools during the same period of time. Again, the scores of the two groups were similar (see Table 4.2): Whether a student had moved from school to school over the years or stayed at Doyle, the average grade-equivalent gains in reading were not significantly different.

These findings contradicted the prevailing attitude that transient students were pulling down the school's test scores. The lack of difference in scores between mobile and stable students showed that poor reading skills were in fact a problem for *both* types of students.

Motivation and Preparedness

The possibility remained that high mobility at Doyle was diminishing the climate for learning for *all* students at the school. If this was the case, negative effects would likely be evident across skill areas and not just in reading, so Jie-Qi conducted an analysis to compare reading, writing, and math scores from the Illinois Goal Assessment Program (IGAP). For this analysis, she used IGAP and not ITBS scores, because the ITBS does not include a writing section. The results indicated that in recent years, the school as a whole had performed better on the writing and math sections of the IGAP than on the reading section. In other words, students' poor performance was not generalized, indicating that they were not completely unmotivated and unprepared, as many teachers believed.

To confirm this set of findings, the probation team conducted a series of observations. From classroom to classroom, they were impressed by the respect and eagerness of Doyle students. Although many students were

TABLE 4.2. The Effects of Multiyear Mobility on Fifth-Graders' ITBS Reading Scores

Group	Average Grade-Equivalent Gain in Reading Scores (1.0 is a gain of 1 year in reading achievement)	Difference in Grade-Equivalent Gains
Fifth-graders who attended Doyle for at least 3 consecutive years (fall 1993–spring 1996)	0.71	0.06
Fifth-graders who attended 2 or more schools between fall 1993 and spring 1996	0.65	

Source: ITBS reading scores provided by the Chicago Board of Education.

Note: The difference in grade-equivalent gains was not found to be statistically significant.

not performing at their grade level in reading, they consistently demonstrated a willingness to learn, trying hard to read whatever was given to them, whether a basal selection, a trade book, or a newspaper article. Renee and Jie-Qi also conducted focus groups with teachers and discovered that on the whole they were more comfortable teaching writing than reading. This was due in part to the school's recent participation in the Illinois Writing Project.

So far, the test score analyses and other assessment activities were suggesting that at Doyle, the low reading scores were attributable less to student characteristics than to classroom practices. To further test this hypothesis, the probation team turned to Jie-Qi for more detailed analyses of ITBS reading scores. First she compared grade-equivalent gains from grade to grade and discovered that intermediate- and upper-grade students had made larger gains than their lower-grade counterparts. This seemed to indicate that lower-grade instructors were not teaching as effectively as others. In addition, she discovered high variation in scores among the lower-grade classrooms themselves: For example, in one second-grade classroom, the average grade-equivalent gain for the 1995–96 school year was 0.72 (about a 7-month gain), while in another second-grade classroom the gain was only 0.1 (about a 1-month gain).

Further analyses by Jie-Qi, this time by skill-specific categories, showed that while upper-level students had better reading scores overall, they, too, had notable weaknesses: They correctly answered a high percentage of test items in the factual-meaning category, but did less well on items measuring inferential and evaluative meaning, which require more higher-order thinking skills than does factual meaning. By this point, the implication of the data analyses was clear: With the same population of students, teachers *can* make a difference, through both what they teach and how they teach.

ENGAGING TEACHERS AND ADMINISTRATORS

When Jie-Qi presented the results of the score analyses to Doyle's teachers and administrators in a specially scheduled meeting, they provoked a debate, because they did not support the belief that students and their families were to blame for the low test scores. Using tables and graphs, Jie-Qi explained the patterns and trends to school staff, helping them to understand the data. Next Renee grounded Jie-Qi's presentation with information gleaned from the classroom observations and focus groups and then opened the floor to questions and discussion.

Because the score analyses were perceived to be objective identifiers of weaknesses and strengths, many teachers shifted from blaming students and parents to recognizing their own need to improve the quality of reading instruction at Doyle. By the end of the presentation, one teacher concluded, "Overall as a faculty we do not know how to teach reading effectively." Far from being dismayed, however, most teachers were grateful for the analyses and presentation. As one teacher said, "This is the first time someone has made a sincere effort to explain the test scores to us and treated us as real professionals. No one has bothered to do this before." Two years later, during the Schools Project evaluation interviews, teachers at Doyle still identified the score analyses as a turning point. One teacher said in an interview:

> Erikson came in and evaluated our school, took the time to lay out the scores and show us what kind of gains we've made. They try to bring in all the factors that we always complain about—the number of students who come and leave our school, the mobility rate, whether or not students have started out at our school. As much as we want to complain about it, as much as we see it as being a problem, and maybe it is in some ways, it doesn't explain the scores.

The presentation of classroom-level data during the meeting was important because it reinforced the idea that individual teachers influence children's outcomes and that they are accountable to the entire school. For the presentation, teachers' names were not attached to their classroom, and although it was possible in some instances to figure out which teachers were linked to which scores by virtue of the number of students in the sample, teachers commented that the approach was not intimidating and made it possible for the faculty to discuss each classroom objectively, without becoming personal. One teacher noted how much the school needed to look critically at itself and that the room-by-room test score analysis was one of the activities that "breathed new life" into the school: "I think we needed to look at them [the scores] that way. . . . It's good to see, depressing as it might have been. It's good to see things laid out that way." In the weeks that followed, Jie-Qi and Renee met with all the teachers individually to discuss the meaning and implications of their students' test scores.

The group presentation also had a corollary effect that the Schools Project had been working toward for years: It helped foster a sense of collective responsibility. "The data exhibit a strong need for collaborative effort in the area of reading! Meetings and sharing among teachers in the same grade level must take place," one faculty member said. Another concurred, "The data indicate that some of our teachers are stronger in specific areas and that we should learn to share our areas/methods of expertise."

In addition, the presentation helped staff articulate for themselves what the general course of the reading intervention should be. Doyle staff responded to the presentation by expressing the need for an intensive schoolwide reading program and more teamwork, in particular. These were exactly the things the probation team had concluded Doyle needed, but instead of imposing them on the staff, they used the presentation to foster self-realization. This had the effect of getting staff more involved as the intervention took shape during the following months, because they felt a sense of ownership. As one researcher pointed out in regard to a different project, "The greatest gains in teacher learning were in place where whole schools studied their student results and agreed on what they needed to know collectively" (Reyni, 1998).

We cannot underplay the extent to which the score analyses fostered teacher engagement in the assessment and intervention process simply because they addressed the issue foremost in their minds at the time—test scores. Teachers in the United States are constantly presented with "new programs" and "innovative approaches," and they are often unresponsive unless they see an immediate and obvious connection to their situation (Feldman, 1998). When test scores are used for accountability purposes, as they are in Chicago, score analyses are more likely than other approaches to capture a school's attention and interest staff in the assessment and intervention process. If it appears that the school and the external partner share the same goal and the same language, the collaboration is more likely to succeed. At Doyle, teachers and administrators felt that Schools Project staff were aware of the importance of standardized test scores for them, and they appreciated that recognition and acknowledgment.

DEVELOPING A READING INTERVENTION

While test score analyses are a useful means for differentiating variables related to students' performance, they do not reveal the specific teaching practices associated with stronger or weaker outcomes. Score analyses are helpful as an assessment tool because they pinpoint areas for further assessment activities of a more qualitative nature, which are necessary to obtain the type of information that can be used to develop an appropriate, focused intervention. To identify the different teaching practices contributing to the varied test scores at Doyle, from grade to grade and also from classroom to classroom within each grade, the probation team carried out a number of investigative tasks, including a teacher survey on reading instruction and observation of individual classrooms.

In general, the classroom observations and survey results were in line with one another. In searching for explanations for the varied scores from grade to grade, the team found that 64% of Doyle's upper-grade teachers were veterans and that they worked more cohesively as a team. In the lower grades, in contrast, only 43% of the teachers were veterans: Among the second-grade teachers, for example, two of the three had little classroom experience. Moreover, there was little collaboration or sharing among the lower-grade teachers. A second-grade teacher whose students had made the least progress in reading, for example, rarely participated in any grade-level meetings, and the other two second-grade teachers did not want to work with him because of "incompatible teaching styles."

From classroom to classroom, the probation team paid special attention to the implementation of the school's existing reading program. Immediately after being put on probation, Doyle administrators had established a school policy that from 9:00 to 10:00 every morning, teachers would focus solely on reading instruction, though specific reading strategies were not outlined. Some form of reading instruction was taking place in most classrooms, but in many of them we observed a host of unrelated activities eating into the instructional hour, including lunch money collections, attendance recording, and announcements.

In observing instructional practices, the team noted several teachers effectively using a range of small-group activities and comprehension strategies, such as reading aloud, thematic mapping, vocabulary development, and story dramatization. In most classrooms, however, whole-group lessons consisting of round-robin reading and responding to factual questions appeared to be the primary method of instruction. Furthermore, many of the teachers using this strategy seemed unaware that students were not engaged.

The observations also revealed that the literacy environment differed dramatically from classroom to classroom. Some had quite a number of trade books creatively displayed and physically accessible to students. In the majority of classrooms, though, the only reading materials to be found were the Great Books series and outdated basal readers.

As part of the assessment activities, Patty conducted interviews at a number of local elementary schools with a demographically similar student population but higher test scores, in order to identify possible factors contributing to the students' better performance. From these interviews, the probation team learned the schools had a few characteristics in common that could be factors in the higher scores, including a comprehensive, well-defined schoolwide reading program; a designated reading coordinator; and a strictly observed daily reading period lasting from an hour to an hour and a half.

In doing the assessment, the team became acutely aware of how much still needed to be done to improve Doyle's reading program, despite the efforts that project staff had already put into the partnership. Over the years, the attention, energy, and resources of Doyle faculty and administrators had been divided and diluted among many different school-improvement projects—at one time, the school had four different external partners— which inevitably limited the impact of any particular project. Thus, while ending up on probation was certainly not a good thing, it did have the benefit of finally focusing Doyle on the literacy objectives that had been important for years.

THE COMPONENTS OF THE INTERVENTION

The probation team did not wait to complete the assessment before starting the intervention; in fact, there was a feedback loop between intervention and assessment activities, including periodic presentations of additional test score analyses (see Chen, Salahuddin, Horsch, & Wagner, 2000, for a more detailed and thorough description of all the test score analyses performed). The intervention consisted of three sets of interrelated activities: (1) training and demonstration, (2) classroom visitations and team planning, and (3) individual consultations and ongoing evaluation. These activities went on for nearly a year and a half, including over the summer. The team's approach to the intervention was typical of other curricular and instructional support provided to partners during the Schools Project, though this time it was embedded in an awareness of the need to raise ITBS reading scores at Doyle to get off probation.

Training and Demonstration

Marie, the team's reading specialist, offered the school a short course on effective reading strategies, which was followed by a series of 10 workshops led by other team members. To build upon existing expertise in the school, they invited experienced teachers to co-lead some of the workshops. In the workshops, the leaders made an effort to link specific reading strategies to the particular skill areas tested by the ITBS; however, while the recommended strategies would help students perform better on the test, they would do so by fostering higher-order thinking skills and overall reading ability. Thus the team was able to address the school's intense focus on the ITBS while avoiding test-driven teaching practices that emphasize discrete, lower-order thinking skills. After the workshops, the team compiled a reading strategy booklet and distributed it to all the teachers.

Next the workshop leaders went to individual classrooms to demonstrate the strategies the teachers had just learned, and following the demonstrations, they met individually with teachers to answer questions and address concerns. Doyle's teachers universally appreciated these visits and wished there was time for even more, as classroom demonstrations and follow-up proved to be one of the most effective ways to translate workshop knowledge into instructional practice.

In addition to the workshop training and demonstration, Renee and Patty helped select and distribute new high-quality books for teachers to build classroom libraries and then organized book talks to help teachers use the libraries. Equipped with effective reading strategies and new materials, Doyle's teachers began to feel more confident about helping their students become better readers.

Classroom Visitations and Team Planning

To establish a sense of professional community at Doyle, Renee arranged a number of classroom observations within the school itself. These visits gave teachers an opportunity to build professional relationships and learn to work collaboratively. After a visit, Renee noticed, teachers showed more interest in writing weekly instructional plans together and experimenting with reading strategies.

Renee also worked with the administration to appoint a veteran teacher to the position of curriculum coordinator. Among her responsibilities, the coordinator was to make sure that grade-level meetings were scheduled regularly and that the meetings promoted collaboration among teachers.

As at other times during the Schools Project, project staff scheduled visits to classrooms in other schools as well, choosing schools with demographically similar students and a successful reading program. What Doyle teachers heard and observed at these other schools underscored the message of the assessment activities: With the same population of students, teachers *can* make a difference. These visits also provided a framework for discussing how the reading intervention could move forward at Doyle, with the other schools serving as models.

Individual Consultations and Ongoing Evaluation

Jie-Qi met with each teacher to review every student's ITBS reading scores, including an analysis by reading skill category, and pinpointed where help was most needed and which strategies were more likely to be beneficial. These individual meetings helped teachers realize that within each classroom there was a diversity of performance levels, and most students had a jagged skill profile as well: That is, the same child might perform extremely differently across the areas of factual, inferential, and evaluative meaning. In presenting these analyses to Doyle faculty, Jie-Qi always reminded them that the reading skills measured through multiple-choice test items on the ITBS do not constitute reading ability; reading involves a much more complex process than can be captured by the isolation of factual meaning, inferential meaning, and evaluative meaning. She emphasized that the skill-area analyses were intended only as a guide to the range of curricular and instructional strategies that should be incorporated in a classroom.

When teachers used new reading strategies in the classroom, Renee teamed up with the school's curriculum coordinator to observe them closely and provide immediate feedback. They also reviewed teachers' instructional plans on a regular basis. These individual consultations were a way to tailor the general reading program being developed at Doyle to the specific needs of each teacher and classroom.

As part of the intervention process, the probation team also worked constantly to evaluate the effectiveness of the new reading initiative. Among the evaluation activities, they regularly observed classrooms and participated in grade-level meetings to determine the impact of the intervention on teachers' attitudes and instructional methods, as well as on student performance. They provided quarterly reports to school administrators and the probation manager, documenting what had been done to build a stronger reading program at Doyle, the progress teachers and students had made, and any concerns or suggestions the team had. And at the end of each academic year, they compared students' test scores to those from previous years and linked their performance to teaching practices. These and other ongoing evaluation activities were critical for monitoring the intervention process and developing specific plans at each step.

GETTING OFF PROBATION

At the end of the 1996–97 school year, a year after Doyle was put on probation, the probation team evaluated the effects of the reading intervention activities to date on the professional development of the faculty and the reading achievement of the students. Through a faculty survey, 85% of the teachers indicated increased knowledge of appropriate reading strategies for their grade level. Team members also observed implementation of a variety of effective strategies in many of the classrooms and noted that most now had a print-rich environment. By the end of the year, grade-level meetings were being scheduled regularly as well; this was due primarily to the appointment of a respected veteran teacher as curriculum coordinator earlier in the year. As teachers became more knowledgeable about effective reading strategies and appropriate materials, these meetings become more productive, providing opportunities for peer collaboration and development of professional community, and they were in part accountable for a more consistent, coherent reading program at Doyle by the end of the year.

These improvements in curriculum and instruction translated into improvements in students' performance on the 1997 ITBS: That year, 18.6% read at or above national norms, a 4.8 percentage point increase over the 1996 score. While still low, this increase was a sign of real progress. Of the 71 elementary schools in Chicago put on probation in 1996, Doyle was one of only 22 to meet or exceed the 15% reading-score standard in 1997.

CPS decided to change the probation standard, however. Now to get off academic probation, at least 20% of Doyle's students had to read at or above national norms, and this became the goal of Doyle's faculty for the next year. Unfortunately, in 1998, students did not make further gains on the ITBS, nor did they sustain the previous year's: The number of students reading at or above national norms dropped to 15.2%.

Doyle was terribly disappointed. The probation team tried to reassure the faculty that test scores can easily fluctuate from year to year at a school, because the forms and levels of the ITBS chosen by the Chicago Board of Education vary from year to year (Bryk, Thum, Easton, & Luppescu, 1998). They also reminded them that although the number of students reading at or above national norms dropped between the first and second years of the intervention, the percentage was still higher than in 1996, when Doyle was put on probation, and higher than in the 6 preceding years.

The team did acknowledge, however, that when scores are as low as those at Doyle, even a drop of a few percentage points warrants close examination, particularly when a school's probation status is determined entirely by the scores. The team decided to organize all the test score data and meet with Doyle's faculty and administrators to try to determine what may have happened during the second year of the intervention to account for the drop in scores.

The review of the 1997–98 academic year revealed a number of circumstances at the school that seem to have contributed to the lack of continued progress that year. These factors included: (1) high turnover among the teachers, (2) the announcement of the principal's retirement, (3) a new probation manager, (4) the resignation of the reading consultant hired for the intervention, and (5) an overemphasis on test practice.

High Turnover Among the Teachers

At the end of the first year of the intervention, in spring 1997, 32% of Doyle's teachers left their jobs; half of them changed jobs because of "the unbearable stress of being at a probation school."

Pressed to replace so many teachers quickly, Doyle administrators had no choice but to hire some new faculty with very little classroom experience. Unfortunately, many of these new teachers were placed in lower-grade classrooms, which had the greatest problems on the ITBS and where effective reading instruction is critical. In addition, these new teachers did not have the benefit of the previous year's training, demonstration, and other intervention activities. Doyle administrators did assign a veteran teacher to lead this cohort of young professionals, but it takes time to mature into a skilled teacher and to understand a school's culture.

The Announcement of the Principal's Retirement

In the middle of the 1997–98 school year, the principal announced her retirement, effective at the end of the year. She had been the principal at Doyle for more than a decade. Many of the faculty members were very attached to her and extremely upset at the announcement of her retirement, particularly as they were in the midst of such a tense probation period.

To make the situation more difficult, the curriculum coordinator, who had been appointed only the year before and who had made such a difference in the grade-level meetings and other intervention activities, had to take over major responsibilities from the principal. She had to write both the school improvement plan and the technology plan, as well as organize and attend a number of school meetings and events. All of this left her little time to focus on curricular and instructional issues. Grade-level meetings occurred only at Renee's suggestion, for example, and even then some teachers did not participate.

A New Probation Manager

At the beginning of the school year, the district assigned a new probation manager to Doyle. It was extremely difficult for the new manager to be dropped into the midst of an intervention already in progress, just as it was hard for new teachers. Also, he had so many other responsibilities for the school district that he had little time to devote to Doyle. Thus a layer of support was missing during the second year of the intervention.

The Resignation of the Reading Consultant

In February 1998, the reading specialist hired to work with the intermediate- and upper-level grades at Doyle resigned in frustration, mostly over lack of cooperation from the new probation manager and some of the teachers. Because it was so late in the academic year, and because it takes time for a consultant to build a relationship with teachers, the team did not replace her, even though this left the intermediate- and upper-grade teachers with less support at the end of the year.

An Overemphasis on Test Practice

After considerable effort among Doyle's teachers to understand the connection between improved test scores and improved classroom practice, they fell back into some old patterns near the end of the 1997–98 school year. About 6 weeks before the ITBS was to be administered, the new probation manager gave a pep talk to the faculty about working harder to improve the school. This was interpreted by the teachers as a push to practice for the ITBS to get scores up. For the next month, from classroom to classroom, teachers spent a significant amount of time teaching test-taking skills and giving practice tests. This type of preparation probably had negative consequences, not only because it pulled students away from curricula that in the long run would provide the surest route to improved scores, but also because it frustrated and wore out the students. After weeks of taking practice tests, many students didn't have the energy or enthusiasm when the day came for the real thing, as a number of teachers noted:

> I have a student walking out of the room 30 minutes after I gave them the test (it is an hour-long testing for that particular section). I asked him to double-check his answers. He said, "I am done. I had enough."

> My students looked so tired on the testing week. I have no idea what's going on with them. Perhaps they were exhausted with all of the testing preparations in the last few weeks. I was, telling you the truth.

A Cumulative Effect

Whenever an intervention is implemented, circumstances are never perfect. During the second year of the reading intervention at Doyle, however, there were so many difficulties and changes, it is hard not to assume that together they were responsible for the lack of progress.

Doyle was at a critical point. Unfortunately, so was the Schools Project: Funding for the project had come to an end. Before our departure, we spoke at length with Doyle's new principal about ways to get back on track. We felt that a strong foundation had been established at Doyle, evident in many teachers' knowledge of the components of a strong reading program, in their motivation to improve their teaching, in changes in their classroom practices, and in their ability to work as a team. The new principal seemed determined to build on this foundation, and we were glad to hear a year later, in the summer of 1999, that Doyle's reading scores had improved enough for the school to be taken off academic probation.

THE REALITY OF HIGH-STAKES TESTING

Few people in the field of education question the importance of school accountability, but many worry that high-stakes testing like that in Chicago will not result in the type of school reform desired (American Educational Research Association, 2000; Haney, 2000; Klein, Hamilton, McCaffrey, & Stecher, 2000; Linn, 2000; Quality Counts, 2001). Despite their concerns, the practice of high-stakes testing has increased, and passage early in 2002 of the No Child Left Behind Act (the legislation to reauthorize the Elementary and Secondary Education Act) actually nationalized the practice, tying failure to meet performance measures on annual reading and math tests to a host of serious consequences for schools and school districts.

In light of this fact, there must be a concerted effort to help administrators and teachers understand the connection between test scores and day-to-day classroom practices, as at Doyle. Without this understanding, score-based accountability systems will not lead to meaningful education reform. For universities, providing this type of assistance to schools may be an important focus for partnerships in the future, as schools seek to improve test scores without resorting to teaching to the test. While the approach we used in the Schools Project is only one way to provide such assistance, there are certain elements of our experience that could be incorporated in any approach.

First, using test-score analyses as the entry point to the assessment and intervention process is probably the most effective way to engage teachers and administrators in improving curriculum and instruction, since it clearly establishes that the external partner acknowledges the crucial role of scores in the life of the school. The analyses are also likely to be perceived as unbiased indicators of factors affecting students' performance on the tests. In the course of identifying the various factors, it is important to distinguish with teachers which ones can be readily addressed through a school-based intervention and which ones the school has virtually no control over.

Second, in the assessment and intervention process, it is important to find ways to foster teachers' sense of both their individual and collective responsibility for school improvement. We have found that individual responsibility is fostered to a large degree through peer review and constructive criticism, as exemplified by the group presentation of the classroom-by-classroom score analyses, while collective responsibility is fostered through teamwork and professional collaboration, such as group planning sessions and classroom visits.

And, finally, implementation of any intervention should be accompanied by ongoing, customized technical assistance and evaluation activities. These activities should involve teachers directly and continuously in a process of learning that will result in improved curriculum and instruction.

CHAPTER 5

The NAEYC Accreditation Process

Building a Strong Foundation for Teaching and Learning

IT WAS ALMOST SIX O'CLOCK in the evening, but the entire pre-kindergarten unit at Nathan School was still ablaze with lights. It had been a memorable day for the pre-K teachers and their assistants: The three classrooms had just received accreditation from the National Association for the Education of Young Children. The official celebration ceremony was over, but people were still gathered in the classrooms, excited and proud. In one room, the principal from Nolan School could be seen congratulating Nathan's principal. Next door, a Nathan teacher was confidently explaining the accreditation process to a group of curious visitors. Touring the classrooms, a teacher from Doyle School murmured, "I think I could do it, too."

That same fall, across the city at Nolan School, two parents were chatting in Spanish. One mother was worried about how her daughter would adjust to preschool: "This is her first school experience, and she speaks little English." "Don't worry," replied the other mother sympathetically. "My daughter was just like yours at the beginning of last year, but she came home from school with a smiley face every day. Oh, I felt so good. She is in kindergarten now. You know, these classrooms just got some kind of license from Washington, D.C. [NAEYC accreditation]. That means they're good ones!"

A year later, Xavier South's child–parent center was celebrating its NAEYC accreditation. At the ceremony, a teacher sighed, "I wouldn't be telling you the truth if I said the process is not hard. It is a hard pill to swallow, but it definitely makes you a better teacher in the end. I now can explain to parents why I am doing the things I'm doing, and why it is good for their children." Echoed Mrs. Rosemary, the child–parent center's head teacher, "This is no easy process, but we worked together and did it. I am so proud of my teachers."

THE VALUE OF NAEYC ACCREDITATION

During the third phase of the Schools Project, we began to encourage partner schools to pursue NAEYC accreditation for their pre-kindergarten and kindergarten classrooms. When CPS started to put schools on probation based on students' standardized test scores, teachers began to feel intense pressure to make sure their students performed well on the test, and they subsequently put pressure on teachers in the grade below to prepare their students better. At the bottom of this chain were the kindergarten and pre-kindergarten teachers, who were asked to do more academic work in their classrooms, focusing in particular on pre-literacy and numeracy skills. Even some parents began to question kindergarten and pre-kindergarten teachers about what they were doing in their classrooms—whether it was really "education."

This pressure made many of the partner schools' preschool teachers deeply uncomfortable. In particular, those who had been involved in the Schools Project in earlier phases believed that their charge was to promote the development of children in all areas—not just their cognitive development, but their social, emotional, and physical development as well. Young children do need to learn the alphabet and to count, but they need to develop other skills, too, such as how to work and play with their peers, how to listen well, how to follow rules, and how to focus on a task. It is also important at this age to foster children's curiosity and their desire to explore, to instill in them a love of school, not fear of it.

It was not enough for us to reassure the pre-kindergarten and kindergarten teachers about the benefits of developmentally appropriate practice. Everyone in these schools, from teachers to administrators to parents, needed to hear a more authoritative voice, and we believed NAEYC could be that voice.

Among the types of accreditation for early childhood programs in the United States, NAEYC accreditation is the most comprehensive and well respected (Anderson, Harvey, & Pinger, 1999; Jacobson, 1999). NAEYC's accreditation standards exceed the requirements for licensing in most states and surpass the standards established by many communities (Bredekamp, 1999; Bredekamp & Willer, 1996; Helburn, 1995; Whitebook, Sakai, & Howes, 1997). For early childhood programs, accreditation from NAEYC lifts them above their counterparts. For parents, NAEYC accreditation provides assurance that their children are in a safe, nurturing environment (Berry & Harris, 1998; Paris, 1998; Smith, 1999).

The principles of developmentally appropriate practice are at the heart of NAEYC accreditation, and we hoped that pursuing accreditation would validate teachers' resistance to a narrow, test-focused approach to early education, in both their own eyes and the eyes of others in the school and community. NAEYC standards assert that by employing a holistic approach in the classroom, by creating a child-centered environment with rich learning opportunities, teachers are creating the strongest foundation for children's future academic success and personal growth (NAEYC, 1998).

Besides supporting developmentally appropriate early education, we believed that the NAEYC accreditation process would draw the pre-kindergarten and kindergarten teachers into the larger professional community. In many public elementary schools, these classrooms are virtually ignored, and this isolation is often exacerbated where high-stakes testing is practiced. "Sometimes I feel that I'm an abandoned, unattended child in the school," said one pre-kindergarten teacher. "I can do whatever I want, because no one cares about what happens here." Many pre-kindergarten and kindergarten teachers even felt isolated from one another.

Through the NAEYC accreditation process, we hoped, schools as a whole would begin to develop a better idea of the fundamental relationship between early childhood classrooms and primary classrooms, and teachers would begin to have a common language for discussing this relationship. Also, as pre-kindergarten and kindergarten teachers pursued accreditation, they were bound to communicate and collaborate more among themselves, to become a more cohesive unit. Their relationship to school administrators was likely to grow stronger and more productive through the process as well.

To promote pursuing NAEYC accreditation in the partner schools, we invited Joan Berger from CPS' early childhood department to join the project. Joan had years of experience as a preschool teacher and early childhood administrator. An experienced NAEYC validator for the accreditation process, she oversaw accreditation for the CPS state pre-K program. We believed that Joan's participation in the project would provide the impetus for partner schools to commit to the accreditation process and also the expertise to guide them through it successfully.

THE NAEYC ACCREDITATION PROCESS
IN THE PARTNER SCHOOLS

The NAEYC accreditation process involves three steps: first a self-study, then validation, and finally the accreditation decision (NAEYC, 1998; as of 2003, the accreditation process and criteria are being reviewed and up-dated by NAEYC). The self-study is conducted by teachers, administra-tors, and parents, who determine how well the program meets NAEYC's criteria for high quality. These criteria address all aspects of early child-hood programs:

- Interactions between staff and children
- Curricula
- Staff–parent interactions
- Administration
- Staff qualifications and development
- Staffing patterns
- Physical environment
- Health and safety
- Nutrition and food service
- Program evaluation

While all these criteria are important, NAEYC places an emphasis on the interactions between staff and children and on the developmental appro-priateness of the curricula.

As part of the self-study, the participants develop and implement a plan to make any improvements necessary to meet NAEYC criteria. Once the program is in compliance with the criteria, participants submit a pro-gram description to NAEYC. The entire self-study process usually takes 9 to 12 months to complete, and it is often quite arduous.

Once the program description has been submitted, one or more trained validators make a site visit to confirm the accuracy of the descrip-tion. After the self-study has been validated and the program director has responded to comments from the validators, a commission comprised of early childhood experts reviews the program description in light of the NAEYC criteria and decides whether accreditation should be granted. If granted, accreditation is for a period of 3 years, during which time the program must submit annual reports documenting continued compliance with the criteria.

For the Schools Project, Joan, along with Renee Salahuddin, Patty Horsch, and Jie-Qi Chen, went from school to school introducing the con-cept of NAEYC accreditation and describing the process. They held gen-eral information sessions for teachers, administrators, and parents and showed a videotape on the accreditation process. After these sessions, re-sponses from teachers covered the entire spectrum, from enthusiasm to flat-out disinterest:

- Sure, why not? I would love to have my classroom accredited by NAEYC.
- How wonderful it would be to get my classroom accredited! Will you help us?
- Okay, well, if we have to, I will.
- No, I'm retiring soon.
- Oh, no. I'm a new teacher, and I don't even know if I can survive this year.
- Why do I have to go through this process? Why do I need it?
- Our school serves an African-American population. Are those standards good for us?
- Who cares about NAEYC accreditation? Kids in these rooms aren't ready to do the work.

While some schools did not immediately commit to pursuing accreditation—they needed more time for consideration—in the end only one of the six schools in the project at the time, Wheaton, decided not to go through the process. Wheaton was on probation, and the principal felt that the teachers didn't need the additional work and pressure. All the other schools, however, embarked on a self-study.

The Self-Study

Classroom observations are the core of the self-study process. NAEYC provides a highly detailed instrument to guide the observations, which were conducted in the Schools Project by Joan Berger; teachers also evaluated themselves using the same instrument. Many teachers were unaccustomed to being observed by an outsider like Joan, particularly as closely as required for the self-study process. Moreover, some teachers were afraid of being reported to the principal if they did not "measure up."

To ease teachers' anxiety, Joan met with them before the initial observation to discuss how it would proceed. She also met with them individually after the initial observation to discuss strengths and weaknesses she had pinpointed and to suggest changes to meet NAEYC criteria. Some teachers were eager for the feedback and support, while others were more sensitive. In many cases, teachers needed some level of assistance to implement changes.

The assistance we provided was attuned to the needs of individual teachers and the culture of the school. In half-day programs, for example, teachers usually needed help figuring out how to provide the full range of NAEYC-recommended learning experiences in such a short amount of time. Or in schools where the administration was less involved in the accreditation process, Joan became the liaison between teachers and the principal, ensuring that teachers received the support they needed for the process to move ahead.

Joan conducted ongoing classroom observations to gauge progress toward meeting NAEYC criteria. She also worked with teachers to balance their self-evaluations against her own observations. Self-evaluations using the classroom observation instrument are required by NAEYC as part of the accreditation process. Sometimes teachers' ratings of themselves were much lower than Joan's, often reflecting their isolation within the school and a lack of respect and validation; other teachers' self-evaluations were higher than Joan's, generally because they misunderstood the criteria or underestimated the level of excellence expected by NAEYC. The purpose of balancing self-evaluations and third-party observations was to develop a consistent understanding among teachers of the NAEYC criteria and to provide a guide for individual teachers in regard to meeting the criteria.

Among the many activities required by NAEYC as part of the self-study, preparing a parent handbook proved surprisingly important and challenging for partner schools. The handbook is supposed to be the primary vehicle for communicating to parents the school's philosophy and policies. Unlike other self-study activities, which tend to be highly structured by NAEYC, creating a parent handbook is open-ended and requires considerable teamwork among teachers. Joan brought samples for the schools to examine, but teachers in each school had to decide consensually what they wanted to include in their handbook. While the partner schools' handbooks all shared certain elements—for example, the goals of the program and the daily schedule—they differed in many respects. One school decided to include a number of more substantive discussions, such as how parents can deal with separation and why play is important in early childhood education. And in two of the schools, separate English and Spanish versions of the handbook needed to be prepared.

Many of the teachers in the partner schools got so involved in the process of evaluating and improving their classrooms during the self-study that they found it difficult to reach the point where they felt ready to prepare the program description and submit it to NAEYC—they felt there was still so much they could do. It was important in these cases for Joan to indicate when she felt a school was ready to submit the program description, while at the same time encouraging teachers to continue with their improvements and growth. As NAEYC (1999) itself has written:

> Achievement of accreditation means that a program has demonstrated substantial compliance with accreditation standards and deserves recognition as a good program. However, it does not mean that the program has com-

pleted the process of making program improvements; accreditation is an
ongoing process of striving for excellence. (p. 4)

Validation

Partner schools had very different validation experiences, as illustrated by
a selection of teacher comments:

- The validator was so pleasant and so wonderful. She made us feel
  so comfortable, because you're nervous about it anyway and you
  want it to go well. She came into the classroom and sat in for a while,
  then she interacted with some of the children. They were showing
  her different things that we were doing. I think she enjoyed that,
  too, because the kids made her part of their life.
- She came in with a positive attitude, very upbeat and very happy
  to be here. I think that made a really big difference. It relaxed me a
  lot, because I was really nervous.
- I had a girl get sick and throw up all over. While I was busy cleaning, one girl asked her to read a book to her, and another child asked
  her to play a puzzle with her. She was very cooperative. I felt kind
  of bad, because I knew how much she had to do in such a short time.
  But she was enjoying herself.
- I heard that she held a strong opinion of the food services we have.
  I don't think she is sensible enough to the situation. Many things
  we are doing here are part of the requirements of the system, and it
  is not possible for a pre-K teacher to make the change.
- She nitpicked at little things, which for me doesn't really have anything to do with what the children are doing. You're not going to
  be always perfect, but you come to evaluate, evaluate the teachers,
  the teacher assistants, the children, not just little things.
- The evaluator? She didn't really have enough time to evaluate certain parts of our schedule. When you did the language arts, she was
  in another room. If you're going to evaluate, you should be more
  thorough. Of course, that wasn't all her fault. One person just could
  not do it all.

This variation was due in large part to the differences among NAEYC
validators in their personal styles and their knowledge of urban public
school systems. Joan and other project staff sometimes served as media-
tors between partner schools and validators during the site visit, particularly when there were circumstances that, within the context of a public
school system, were impossible to change. One school, for example, is lo-

cated in an unsafe neighborhood, which prevents children from going outdoors to play—teachers would be putting students at risk by sending them outside. Another school has no playground at all and nowhere to build one. These circumstances make it impossible for the two schools to meet the NAEYC criterion for daily outdoor playtime. Another example involves the NAEYC requirement to keep certain documents on site at the school. Many of the required documents, including confidential person-nel files, are kept at the CPS central office.

We discussed these sorts of issues with the validators to ensure that the schools applying for accreditation were given fair consideration. Many of the NAEYC validators were more accustomed to evaluating child care settings than early education programs in public schools, and sometimes criteria had to be interpreted from a different perspective.

Accreditation

All of the classrooms in the partner schools that pursued NAEYC accredi-tation with assistance from the Schools Project were granted it—18 pre-kindergarten and kindergarten classrooms in five schools. Because these classrooms were among the first in the Chicago public school system to pursue NAEYC accreditation, they have become an inspiration for other CPS teachers to undertake the process. Certainly the success of the partner schools is a testament to the commitment of the teachers, administrators, and parents who undertook the self-study and worked to meet NAEYC's stan-dards of high quality. Credit is also due to Joan Berger, who worked with the partner schools from the beginning to the end of the accreditation pro-cess. Besides providing customized assistance at every step based on the specific needs and circumstances of each school and each teacher, she also worked to develop leadership within each school and, true to the enabling approach, encouraged participants to identify goals themselves.

Joan herself received support from the rest of the Schools Project team, particularly during the biweekly project meetings. Project staff who were intimately involved in the schools in other areas of intervention could pro-vide guidance during the accreditation process and even join in when ad-ditional assistance was necessary.

Over and over again, teachers cited Joan's participation in the ac-creditation process as critical to their success. They are not alone in rec-ognizing the importance of technical assistance in achieving NAEYC accreditation. An independent evaluation of the process and outcomes of NAEYC accreditation indicates that intensive support, including on-site technical assistance and customized training for staff, helps programs achieve accreditation at more than twice the rate of programs that do not receive such support (Whitebook, Sakai, & Howes, 1997). This finding, coupled with the experience of the Schools Project, suggests that NAEYC accreditation might be a particularly fruitful goal for university–school partnerships.

HOW THE NAEYC ACCREDITATION PROCESS
CHANGED PARTNER SCHOOLS

Pursuing NAEYC accreditation now tops the list of strategies to upgrade care and education programs for young children (Bredekamp, 1999; Carter-Blank & Jor'dan, 1999; Whitebook, Sakai, & Howes, 1997). This indeed proved true for partner schools, which saw marked changes over the course of the accreditation process. There were four general areas of growth for the pre-kindergarten and kindergarten classrooms that pursued accreditation: (1) the development and strengthening of common goals among teachers in regard to developmentally appropriate education; (2) improvements in classroom practice; (3) decreased isolation and increased collaboration among teachers; and (4) closer school–parent relationships.

The Development and Strengthening of Common Goals Among Teachers

If teachers are going to pursue NAEYC accreditation, they must agree with the principles of developmentally appropriate education, which are central to NAEYC criteria. As in any school, however, the partner schools had pre-kindergarten and kindergarten teachers with diverse ideas about children and pedagogy. One teacher, for example, initially argued strongly in favor of a focus on pre-academic skills and seatwork. She said, "These children need structure. . . . Many parents are not able to do much to help these kids academically. If we don't do it, how would these kids get ready for primary school?" In her opinion, developmentally appropriate practice was not the best strategy for poor minority children.

Other teachers countered strongly. One responded:

> The primary [mode of] instruction for poor children and Black children nowadays is ditto sheets and drills, because it is believed to be good for them to develop basic skills. I don't buy that. If we don't help these poor minority children develop self-initiation, independent thinking skills, they are never going to manage their own lives well—and forget about being the leaders of tomorrow.

Another teacher offered a similar opinion: "Academic readiness should not be just basic skills from drill and practice. I have different learning centers where the children learn through play, exploration, and interaction with peers. They are certainly learning, and learning in a fun way."

Still another teacher argued, "Don't forget that young children, Black or White, poor or rich, learn from the concrete to the abstract, not the reverse. The poorer the kids are, the less likely [it is that] they get manipulatives, books at home to support their concrete learning, so all the more we need to provide rich learning experiences to them."

Through group discussions, teachers examined the theories and values underlying developmentally appropriate education and reflected on their own practices and beliefs. We guided these discussions and made sure that people felt safe to express their points of view. By acquiring a deeper understanding of developmentally appropriate practice, in tandem with exploring their own personal experiences and attitudes, teachers began to move toward common ground in thinking about how best to support individual children in the classroom and, in turn, why to pursue NAEYC accreditation. As one teacher described the experience, "Before this, we all had our own things [we believed] and we each probably did [things] differently in the classroom. Through this process, we argued, compared our thoughts, and finally put a booklet together. We're together now because we share a similar philosophy." This experience represents professional development at the most profound level, where practice begins to change not because of external demands, but because of internal shifts in understanding and belief.

Improvements in Classroom Practice

It is impossible to pinpoint which facets of the accreditation process most directly improved classroom practice, but NAEYC's classroom observation instrument, along with Joan Berger's feedback after observations, certainly played a significant role. As one teacher noted, with such a comprehensive and detailed checklist, "You couldn't help but have a better room just from doing it."

The observation instrument goes in depth in five main areas—health and safety, nutrition, physical environment, interactions between staff and children, and curricula—and teachers found it extremely helpful. For some, it simply confirmed that they were already on the right track: "I'm glad I went through this process. I know that my practices did not really change much because I was already doing it. But it's good to know that you're doing the right thing, concerning children." For others, it opened their eyes to new ways of doing things in the classroom: "Those handouts that we had to rate ourselves brought out a lot of my weaknesses, and showed me areas I need to work on and develop. It helped me with skills I didn't know were important at the time. I had to rethink my lessons and make them more conducive to the preschool children."

There are many specific examples of how teachers and classrooms changed during the accreditation process. Teachers looked very closely at their physical spaces and made improvements. At the most basic level, they made sure that classrooms were free of hazards and kept clean. "This made us get little things that we knew we should have," said a teacher, "like a fire extinguisher, a first aid kit, hiding chemicals and detergents, and locked cabinets. The process made us more aware of safety issues and taking care of the environment." Teachers also began to rearrange their classrooms to better meet the needs of young children: "Also room arrangement, like I had a piano in the middle of the room, and I didn't want to move it. Once I did, it made my room look even bigger. Little things like that, we resist. I've been a teacher for a really long time, so it's really hard to change." And more of the children's artwork began to be displayed in the classrooms, along with photos of family and classroom events. As a teacher noted, "The room belongs to the children, not to the teacher."

In thinking about how to foster children's physical development, teachers began to pay greater attention to the balance between quiet and active time during the day, as well as between indoor and outdoor activities. In one school, the early childhood teachers lobbied to expand the playground so that children would have room to ride bikes when outside.

There were also noticeable changes in the way teachers thought about the social and emotional development of their young students. When dealing with behavioral problems, instead of yelling at children or simply ignoring the disruption, teachers began to take a more proactive approach to developing children's capacity for self-control and teaching them that they are responsible for their actions: "I have a lot of children that need a lot of strong discipline and guidance. I think it [the accreditation process] showed me ways of how to think and how to react to these children in a more positive light than 'No, don't do this.'" Instead of employing punitive methods, such as time-outs, calls to parents, or suspensions, teachers became more inclined to actively involve children in making classroom rules and to use stories, children's literature, and mini-lessons to illustrate proper behavior. Teachers reported that other changes in their classrooms also contributed to a decrease in behavioral problems; these changes included more diverse learning activities, a more engaging environment, and greater attention to individual children.

In regard to curriculum and instruction, worksheets and chalkboard lessons were largely replaced by learning centers and hands-on opportunities for learning, and teachers became conscious of balancing self-directed and structured activities. They also began to take time to observe individual children more closely, in order to uncover their unique learning profiles. "In my room, I let the children do more hands-on things," reported a teacher. "I allow them to be more independent. They make choices on their own. I just try to redirect them as needed. Once they know what they're supposed to do, I can go around and observe them, what they do and how they do it." Because of the broader range of learning opportunities, teachers became more likely to notice students' individual strengths, not just their weaknesses, and were able to build on those strengths. Some teachers reported that they began to believe more in each child's ability to learn and shine.

The NAEYC accreditation process also resulted in more multicultural curricula. In particular, two partner schools with Afrocentric curricula began to include other cultures:

> You know, our school is Afrocentric, completely Afrocentric. We have been working so hard on being Afrocentric, because we're raising the self-esteem of our children. As a result of the accreditation process, we are aware that we need to be a little more multicultural. We've been bringing some other things into our curriculum.

All these changes in classroom practice did not come at the cost of children's acquisition of basic academic skills. Children came out of the accreditation classrooms knowing their letters, understanding basic numeric concepts, and recognizing colors, plus they exhibited a host of other positive qualities: They tended to be active learners, they were better able to focus, and they were better behaved. At one of the partner schools, several first-grade teachers who taught children coming out of accredited classrooms specifically commented on this accomplishment: "Those kids were good. They listened well and exhibited fewer behavioral problems. They also know the basics. We wish we could do the same thing for these children as the teachers in the pre-K and kindergarten classrooms did."

Decreased Isolation and Increased Collaboration Among Teachers

In addition to validating and supporting developmentally appropriate early education, the NAEYC accreditation process succeeded in building professional community. In pursuing accreditation, teachers from different classrooms began to work together more than they ever had before. At

Nathan, for example, the three pre-kindergarten teachers visited one another informally almost every day and also met formally as needed. At Nolan, the pre-kindergarten and kindergarten teachers formed a committee on classroom behavior problems: If a teacher had a child with a special behavioral issue, the committee members would conduct an observation together, talk with the child's parents, and then make a group decision about what to do. At Xavier South, Mrs. Rosemary, the head teacher at the child–parent center, worked closely with her faculty to design an appropriate classroom environment and curriculum activities, and the weekly staff meeting became a forum for solving common problems and learning new teaching strategies. In all the schools, preparation of the parent handbook was a group effort, and it gave teachers a chance to appreciate one another's strengths as they divvied up the tasks: Some collected information, some typed the handbook, some translated it. All these collaborative activities led to a strong sense of community among teachers, helped them learn from one another, and gave them a cross-classroom perspective.

Collaboration was not always easy, however. One teacher described her experience: "Everybody started saying, 'You need this, you need that.' I learned to accept it because it was constructive criticism." Echoed another teacher, "At first it was hard to hear your colleagues' disapproving comments. As we say, old habits die hard, changing is not that easy. But hearing a different voice forced you to look back at what you have done." The collaborative nature of the NAEYC accreditation process forced teachers to be self-reflective, as they constantly encouraged and challenged one another to consider the impact of their actions on children and parents, and vice versa.

At Doyle School, there was only a single classroom going through the accreditation process, so the experience was somewhat different. But the teacher and her assistant built a sense of professional community their own way, by talking to teachers in other grades at the school and by visiting classrooms in other partner schools pursuing accreditation.

Another positive consequence of the accreditation process was that it promoted communication and mutual understanding between early childhood teachers and the school principal, since it was impossible to go through the process without administrative support:

> [Our principal] was supportive of us going through the process. If we said, "We need three first aid kits," he would say, "Fine, go buy them." This year each of our pre-kindergarten and kindergarten classrooms had a new rug. We also had more children's books and manipulatives, thanks to the support of our principal.

Administrative support also often led to improved relations between pre-school teachers and other teachers in the school. "The principal told everybody in our faculty meeting what I was doing and why it was important," said a teacher. "In the next few days, several upper-grade-level teachers came to my classroom. They wanted to see what a NAEYC classroom could look like." Upon accreditation, the whole school celebrated the achievements of the preschool classrooms.

Closer School–Parent Relationships

NAEYC considers strong school–parent relationships to be a critical element of high-quality programs, so parents are an integral part of the accreditation process. In the partner schools, parents were informed about the decision to pursue NAEYC accreditation at the beginning of the process, through both parent conferences and a newsletter.

Along with teachers and administrators, parents undertake the self-study, evaluating how well their children's program meets NAEYC criteria. There is a separate parent questionnaire for the self-study, and in the partner schools it presented several challenges. First, most parents had never before been asked to evaluate their children's classrooms, and they felt very awkward and worried that they would offend the teachers. Second, many of the questions were difficult to understand, either because they were poorly worded or because they were more applicable to a child care setting than a public school classroom. And third, many parents had low literacy skills or did not speak English, which intensified the comprehension problems.

The teachers made a huge effort to overcome these barriers. Some wrote explanatory notes next to hard-to-understand questions, such as "This sentence means . . . ," "What they really mean here is . . . ," "This does not apply to our program," and "Please look at page 7 of the parent handbook for this question." Others set up meetings with three or four parents at a time to explain the questionnaire; for parents who did not speak English, teachers would translate each question. Parents then took the questionnaire home to complete it. All these activities around the questionnaire served to strengthen teacher–parent relations, by showing teachers' willingness to work with parents, by helping parents develop a better understanding of what teachers were trying to do in the classroom, and by communicating to parents that their opinions are important.

Working on the questionnaire inspired many parents to become more involved in the accreditation process and in their children's education, particularly as their understanding of teachers' goals and practices grew. At Nathan, for example, many parents started reading to their children every evening. At Xavier South, a group of parents began volunteering regularly in the classroom. And parents in many of the schools would do things like come early in the morning on the day of the validators' visit to help teachers clean the classrooms.

Another aspect of the accreditation process that led to improved school–parent relations was preparation of the parent handbook. As teachers decided what to include in their school's handbook, they had to carefully consider the children's parents—what would be most helpful for them to know, how they could be involved at school, what languages the handbook should be in, and other questions. Teachers sought parent input for the handbooks, and many parents offered suggestions. For teachers, working on the handbooks gave them a deeper understanding of the families and communities they served, and when the handbooks were completed, they served as a bridge between school and home: The handbooks clearly explained the philosophy and goals of the early childhood programs; gave important information on day-to-day operations, including phone numbers, schedules, policies, and procedures; and described opportunities for parent involvement at school and at home. For many parents, the handbook was important not just because of the information it contained, but also because it acknowledged them as true partners in the education of their children.

A teacher at one of the partner schools perfectly summarized how NAEYC accreditation led to improved school–parent relationships: "This accreditation process really helped bring the parents and us together. Parents now know what we are doing and that what we are doing is good for their kids. And they are supporting us and trying to do the same things at home." Parents felt the same way, as one mother enthusiastically recounted:

> Teachers worked very hard for letting us know what's going on in the classroom and with my child. They talked to me at the door when I picked up my child, and they let me sit in the classroom to see what my child was doing. I feel comfortable with them. . . . They have gone through an accreditation process. I support them 100% and I know they will get [accreditation].

CHAPTER 6

The Responsive Classroom Approach

A Caring, Respectful School Environment as a Context for Development

AS THE SCHOOLS PROJECT APPROACHED its seventh year, teachers in the partner schools, particularly Nolan, began to express a new set of concerns. While generally pleased with the DAP-based methods of instruction they were learning through the Schools Project, teachers were troubled by students' underdeveloped social skills and lack of academic initiative. Meanness and aggression erupted often among children, disrupting learning time, and even students whose conduct was good were frequently unfocused and disengaged. These problems had always existed, but they became more pronounced as teachers shifted toward child-centered instructional strategies, whose success required a higher degree of social-emotional maturity and self-motivation among students than the success of traditional strategies.

Children's negative behaviors usually originated outside the classroom—stressful events at home, an unresolved playground conflict, even lack of sleep or poor health. The routines of pencil-and-paper tasks had limited the opportunities for children to act out, but the more cooperative and open methods of learning made it easier for their feelings to overflow in the classroom. "I'm not going to work with him" was heard often when groups were formed for activities. "Ooh, you got that wrong" became a familiar insult when a child made a mistake at the blackboard. Or when assignments were returned, it was not unusual to hear one student say to another, "You dummy, you only got one right." Children more and more frequently could be heard making derogatory comments about their classmates, and teachers began to feel they were more often in the role of conflict mediator than learning facilitator. With their new understanding of developmentally appropriate practice gained through the project, teachers were hesitant to employ punitive methods of discipline, yet most had no other strategies to fall back on.

The new instructional approaches teachers were using also highlighted how unprepared or unwilling children were to be a partner in the learning process and assume age-appropriate responsibilities. When teachers were introducing an activity using new materials, for example, many students would dart for the supplies before the introduction was finished and they understood their purpose. In group activities, many children also had trouble understanding what their role should be: Some would disrupt the group, while others would sit silent. "It's not fair" and "She won't do her part" were common laments.

All in all, teachers were at a loss for ways to help students develop the capacity to act in a caring, respectful manner toward their classmates or for ways to create a classroom atmosphere that would make children feel safe and supported, enabling them to focus on their work and take the risks necessary for learning. Moreover, the circumstances in which most teachers worked made any efforts that much harder: Classes were generally large and multilingual; often there were inadequate instructional supplies and no teacher aides; and many students had particularly serious social, emotional, and cognitive problems. Also, the pressures of high-stakes testing, which had taken hold in the Chicago Public Schools by this point in the project, left teachers wondering how they could find time in the already packed required curriculum to teach social competencies— skills not assessed by the board of education. "Help us resolve our dilemma," a Nolan teacher said to Patty Horsch during a Schools Project meeting, and others echoed her plea.

FINDING THE RIGHT TOOLS TO SUPPORT STUDENTS' SOCIAL-EMOTIONAL DEVELOPMENT

From research and experience, we knew that a caring, respectful classroom environment would strengthen students' sense of belonging, thereby motivating them to identify with the goals of the school; conversely, a classroom environment of criticism and disapproval would have a negative effect on achievement (Lewis, Schaps, & Watson, 1996; Schaps, Battistich, Solomon, & Watson, 1997). But we also knew that a caring, respectful environment alone is not enough: When teachers are academically focused— providing clear instruction, ensuring opportunities for practice and feedback, and structuring time for real engagement in tasks—students achieve more (Brophy & Good, 1986; Darling-Hammond, 1998; Darling-Hammond & Sclan, 1996; National Commission on Teaching and America's Future, 1996).

After a review of models to support young students' social-emotional development, we suggested the Responsive Classroom approach to the partner schools. Developed by the Northeast Foundation for Children, the Responsive Classroom strives to develop in students an "ethical ideal," the desire and knowledge to act in more caring ways (Charney, 1991, 1997). The approach has six components: Morning Meeting, Rules and Logical Consequences, Guided Discovery, Classroom Organization, Academic Choice, and Assessment and Reporting to Parents. These components work both alone and in concert to help students develop the social skills of cooperation, assertion, responsibility, empathy, and self-control and also to promote in them a deeper knowledge of academic subject areas, reasoned decisionmaking, and motivation for learning (Charney, Clayton, & Wood, 1995). Overall, the components are consonant with the theories underlying developmentally appropriate educational practice (Bredekamp & Copple, 1997; Charney, 1991; Charney, Clayton, & Wood, 1995) and therefore were in keeping with the philosophy of the Schools Project.

Morning Meeting

This daily ritual builds a sense of community while setting a positive tone for the day. Its four elements—greeting, sharing, a group game or activity, and a daily letter with news from the teacher—provide an opportunity for children to learn and practice a variety of social and academic skills, including speaking in front of others about meaningful experiences, listening to peers and responding appropriately with questions and comments, working cooperatively, and using knowledge recently learned in class (for example, new vocabulary words or numeric tasks). The supportive atmosphere of Morning Meeting makes it easier for children to take the risks necessary to master these skills.

Rules and Logical Consequences

These classroom management tools are designed to promote and sustain a sense of community and instill "habits of goodness" in children (Charney, 1997). Developed at the beginning of the school year by the teacher and students together, rules are positive statements that establish guidelines and expectations for behavior; they are the cornerstone of classroom life and are used to encourage conversation and problem-solving related to ethical issues that arise in school. Examples of classroom rules include "Respect yourself," "Respect others," and "Respect the environment."

Logical consequences are nonpunitive responses to student wrong-doing. They are designed to be situation- and child-specific. A child who has broken someone's pencil while trying to grab it, for example, might be required to replace the pencil with a new one from home. Logical consequences are meant to support children as they learn to behave in socially responsible ways and to help them make amends and soothe feelings when they've hurt someone.

Guided Discovery

This is a process for introducing classroom materials (for example, games, art supplies, books, and computers) and learning methods (for example, writing or reading workshops) to students in a way that generates their excitement and invites their active participation in constructing knowledge about the potential and use of the materials and methods. A Guided Discovery incorporates modeling and demonstration to teach skills and concepts, but it goes even further. The interactive process between students and the teacher includes naming the object or learning activity to establish a common vocabulary, generating ideas about its potential and use, actively exploring the ideas with the group, and making decisions about the care of materials. During a Guided Discovery, students also learn and practice social skills that promote cooperative learning, such as listening to one another, appreciating one another's ideas, asking thoughtful questions, and making respectful comments. Materials and methods introduced through a Guided Discovery are subsequently made available for student use in the classroom.

Classroom Organization

In a Responsive Classroom, the physical space is organized to both maximize children's independence and facilitate peer interactions, whether for partners, a small group, or the entire class. A carpeted area or open space invites the whole group to gather and see one another face to face, for example, and tables around the room or specific interest areas offer opportunities for partner or small-group interactions.

The physical environment should also contribute to the development of a classroom culture, constructed by the students and teacher together over time. A part of the classroom, for example, might be set aside for the display of student projects completed as part of the science curriculum. As the class moves through the curriculum, new projects are continually added to the display, alongside earlier projects. Over the months, the display becomes a representation to the children of their progress through the curriculum and their growing body of knowledge and achievement.

Academic Choice

Giving children choices at school helps them develop a sense of owner-ship in regard to the learning process. In a Responsive Classroom, students are regularly given the opportunity to make choices about their own learn-ing. The teacher presents options or provides guidance for choosing a topic of study or a method or materials for a project. The choice might be as simple as a book for independent reading or as complex as a semester-long research project.

Assessment and Reporting to Parents

Ongoing home–school communication is critical for a productive rapport between parents and teachers; it helps both parties understand how best to promote children's academic learning and social-emotional develop-ment. The Responsive Classroom approach recommends that teachers ini-tiate the first contact with parents early in the school year. Teachers should invite parents to share their concerns and goals for their child, and teach-ers should express their own as well. They should also communicate that parents are welcome in the classroom at any time. The guidelines for the Responsive Classroom approach suggest many activities for parents, both those who help out in the classroom regularly and those who visit only occasionally or spontaneously.

CREATING A CARING, RESPECTFUL COMMUNITY: FOUR CASE HISTORIES

After introducing a partner school to the Responsive Classroom approach, we arranged for interested teachers to attend an introductory 3-day work-shop led by trainers from the Northeast Foundation for Children. In some cases, the workshop was also attended by teacher assistants, administra-tors, and even parents. The participants watched demonstrations and vid-eos, role-played, and discussed the literature provided by the trainers. They learned the nuts and bolts of the approach: for example, how to devise Rules and Logical Consequences, how to conduct Morning Meetings, and how to lead Guided Discoveries. They explored and practiced using "effective" language—language that reminds, redirects, and reinforces—and discussed the need to model desired social behaviors.

After teachers began to implement the Responsive Classroom approach in their own schools, with follow-up support from us, some decided to get advanced training from the Northeast Foundation for Children. Additionally, leadership teams of administrators and teachers from four of the partner schools attended a weeklong Responsive Leadership Institute offered by the foundation. Through its work with schools around the country, the foundation has come to recognize that the Responsive Classroom approach is most successful when the philosophy is applied to everyone in a school, children and adults alike, so that the entire school becomes a caring community. The leadership institute is intended to help teachers and administrators move toward this goal. Participants have the opportunity to step outside their formal school roles and experience firsthand what it is like to be part of a responsive learning community. Among the many activities during the week, participants collaboratively formulate plans for supporting the adults in their schools; discuss guidelines for setting schoolwide disciplinary policies and the possible pitfalls as the policies are implemented; and devise ways to evaluate student and school outcomes resulting from the Responsive Classroom approach. For the Schools Project, Patty Horsch and Renee Salahuddin attended the institute with the leadership teams, which permitted them to get to know the school leaders more deeply and to become more integral members of the school community.

Evaluations of the training workshop and leadership institute by Schools Project participants were consistently high, and everyone who attended was filled with enthusiasm and determination. Despite these auspicious signs, no other intervention during the project ended up looking so different from school to school as the Responsive Classroom. At one extreme, an entire school community—students, teachers, administrators, even parents—was transformed. At the other extreme, teachers in a couple of the schools came to see the approach as little more than an ivory-tower program unsuitable for inner-city children. The four brief case histories in this section convey the range of experiences among the partner schools, and they serve as a springboard for a more general discussion of the intervention's effects in the last section of the chapter.

Nolan School: Theory into Practice, Perfectly

As you enter Nolan, a welcome message taped to the wall greets you. Original student work from every classroom lines the halls: book reports, science projects, paintings and drawings, essays on what it means to be "me." The principal speaks to children by name, telling them she's sorry she couldn't come out to jump rope yesterday, but she'll be there today. In each room, a brightly colored rug provides a space for everyone to gather; bookcases and pillows mark the library corner; and there are learning centers that children use during designated times of the day for reading, playing board games, or working on individual and group projects.

Even though the bell hasn't rung yet, many children are already in their classrooms, excited and full of energy. In a first-grade classroom, several students have gathered around the News and Announcements chart, where they are trying to figure out the answer to the question of the day: How many words are in the daily message? "There are thirty-six!" "I think there are five!" "These are the words, the ones with spaces between them." The discussion continues until their teacher calls the students to the rug for Morning Meeting. In a rhyming chant, they welcome each other to class. A noncompetitive game follows, to build group spirit and heighten the enjoyment of being in school. Then the teacher leads the class through the News and Announcements letter, helping the children decode the words as they discover the exciting plans for the day.

In a fifth-grade classroom, Morning Meeting looks somewhat different—it's more appropriate for older children—but the ritual has the same comfortable feeling. Monday through Thursday, students plan and lead Morning Meeting, including writing and reading the News and Announcements letter. On Fridays, the teacher leads the class in a new song or activity. This carefully crafted shift in power nurtures student responsibility.

At the end of the Schools Project, teachers at Nolan considered the Responsive Classroom the most important initiative they had undertaken. Their exceptional experience with the approach might have been predicted from the outset. They were the most insistent among the partner schools in asking for help to address children's social-emotional development, and our first step was to invite interested teachers to participate in a critical exploration of the ideas behind the Responsive Classroom. The 12 teachers who chose to get involved at this stage, representing about a third of Nolan's faculty, were asked to read *Teaching Children to Care: Management in the Responsive Classroom* (Charney, 1991), and a number of before-school meetings were scheduled to discuss the book. The teachers' efforts were wholly supported by the principal, who provided stipends for the time spent in the meetings.

Over the course of reading and discussion, teachers became excited about the approach. It focused on the whole child. It validated the kinds of behaviors valued by the school. Importantly, it interwove development of social skills with academic instruction: Teachers were already coping with a school day too short to cover the curricular material required by the Chicago Public Schools, and there was no time to implement a separate social skills curriculum. During discussion sessions, we facilitated teachers' reflection on the compatibility between the Responsive Classroom approach and their own pedagogical beliefs. For this group, the approach was an almost perfect fit.

Following this introduction to the Responsive Classroom, nine teachers, two special education teachers, the librarian, and the assistant principal (who later became the principal) joined teachers from another partner school for their initial training from the Northeast Foundation for Children. When school started in the fall and the teachers began to implement the approach in their classrooms, we provided technical support, but from the beginning Nolan's teachers took ownership, working hard to find ways to make the new strategies work for them and their students.

That winter, Nolan's staff gathered for a midyear evaluation of new initiatives at the school, including the Responsive Classroom. Patty Horsch led the session. One teacher remarked that it was taking a lot of time to create a caring community. This comment was interpreted by Patty as criticism of the Responsive Classroom, and she categorized it on a flip chart as a negative response. "No, no, no," the teacher interjected. "That is just a fact. It is not a negative. The Responsive Classroom really works." Other teachers joined her in support of the intervention, and the physical education teacher and the librarian both commented that they already perceived a noticeable difference in students whose teachers were implementing the approach. These students exhibited more caring behaviors, were more cohesive as a class, and were generally calmer and more ready to learn.

The principal took note, and when the new school improvement plan was drawn up, schoolwide implementation of the Responsive Classroom approach was a central feature. The administration was committed to cultivating the values of a caring, respectful community throughout the entire school. During the summer, all of Nolan's teachers and staff attended a weeklong training workshop, and when school started in the fall, the daily schedule was reconfigured so that every student, as well as all ancillary staff, would participate in a classroom Morning Meeting.

Mandates are not in keeping with the enabling approach, and we worried that the Morning Meeting requirement might actually hurt the initiative. At Nolan, it did not. Most teachers had a deep understanding of the Responsive Classroom approach, and it meshed with their own goals, so even those who found the new schedule inconvenient adjusted to it. For Nolan, the mandate actually unified the school even further, instead of creating divisions. "I think the school is very connected now that every teacher in the school has been trained in Responsive Classroom," said a teacher. "Everyone from nine o'clock to nine-thirty does a common thing in the school no matter if you are kindergarten or sixth grade." Another teacher reinforced this view:

> There is a sense of unity. Everyone does their own thing, but there is one thing that we all do at the same time, and it also involves nonclassroom teachers. Everyone must be involved. So I think that one thing provides unity. I don't mean uniformity as in behavior modification.

Misbehavior did not disappear entirely at Nolan with the introduction of the Responsive Classroom, but teachers' responses to it changed dramatically. Their responses demonstrated their trust in children's ability to grow and improve and also their own willingness to help children along. When students hurt others' feelings, teachers helped them salve relationships through an "apology of action," which offered a reparation for the misdeed. When one student insulted a classmate, for example, his apology of action was to make a card for the child. When presented to the student, the genuinely funny card made her laugh. A lesson was taught and a relationship restored. At Nolan, 100% of teachers surveyed said that the Responsive Classroom approach had influenced their classroom interactions with students.

In turning the whole of Nolan into a caring community, it was important that the administration modeled the principles of the Responsive Classroom in interactions with staff and students. Sometimes they even incorporated elements of Morning Meeting into faculty meetings to build collegiality and interdependence.

Parents of Nolan students were introduced to the Responsive Classroom approach during PTA and Local School Council meetings. They were extremely supportive of the approach, especially as they began to notice changes at home. One mother described how her first-grader prepared a News and Announcements letter for his family on a Saturday morning. Another parent commented, "I was so happy to see Nicole at our door one Sunday morning to work with my daughter on a science project. The sense of community created by the Responsive Classroom has made this happen." Parents uniformly expressed appreciation that the school was helping to break down social and racial barriers between children, allowing them to make new friends.

One teacher summed up the school's experience with the Responsive Classroom approach: "Definitely the Responsive Classroom has added a wonderful dimension for the school, for reaching the whole child."

Trujillo School: The Toll of Teacher Turnover

Soon after the school joined the project in 1995, Trujillo's principal left for another position. A new principal was chosen by Chicago's school reform board, but the choice deeply divided staff, and over the next few years many teachers left the school, including a large number of those who had received Responsive Classroom training from the Northeast Foundation for Children. Each fall, new teachers started at the school who knew nothing about the approach.

The new principal was committed to implementing the Responsive Classroom schoolwide, but Trujillo was placed on academic probation soon after she started, and she had to make hard choices about how to spend time and money. Instead of sending new faculty to a weeklong training course or organizing one on-site, the principal decided to institute a 45-minute weekly meeting before school during which Renee Salahuddin, the main project staff person at Trujillo, worked with all of the school's faculty on the Responsive Classroom approach. The fact that all teachers were required to attend these meetings presented a host of challenges, as Renee tried to meet the very different needs of those who were already using the approach in their classrooms and those who were just learning about it. To make matters worse, a variety of circumstances prevented the meetings from occurring on a weekly basis until the second semester, leaving the new teachers with a mandate to implement the Responsive Classroom, but little information or support to do so.

Even when the meetings became regular, many teachers expressed a desire for more in-depth training. "We are supposed to meet on Thursdays, and we do get some training," said one teacher. "We do, but I don't think it is enough. I think we should do an all-day thing." During the weekly meetings, there was no time for meaningful collaboration among colleagues or reflection on personal practice.

Resource constraints were not the only problem at Trujillo, however. Tensions between the new administration and some teachers had an effect on the initiative as well, as a teacher articulated:

> I think if you're going to make the Responsive Classroom as the base for what our school is about, make it consistent not only with the students but among the staff and with the teachers. For example, I'm a new teacher here. When I walk into the building, sometimes I walk right in front of the office. Who says good morning? Nobody. How does that make a teacher feel? It doesn't make me feel welcome. I can see that if I did that to my students, if I just ignored them and let them come in, how is that going to make them feel?

The new principal hoped that the weekly training meetings would bring the adult community at Trujillo closer together. Ironically, the rift only widened when some veteran teachers refused to attend the meetings. They felt that the meetings merely repeated the training they had already received and provided no time to reflect on implementation issues with which they were dealing. They were also frustrated by the fact that school administrators failed to model caring behaviors in their interactions with staff and children.

Despite all these problems, many teachers at Trujillo saw value in the Responsive Classroom approach. Morning Meeting provided an effective way for teachers to welcome children who had traveled across the city to get to school and to help them settle in for the day, and teachers spoke enthusiastically about the ways that Guided Discoveries helped children take ownership in the classroom and accept more responsibility. In describing the effects of the Responsive Classroom, one first-grade teacher said, "The children know the right thing to do, they are happy. The behavior of the children is better, and they are more engaged in classroom routines. I am happy, too. I feel more comfortable with myself and more confident as a teacher."

Trujillo's new principal continued to view the Responsive Classroom approach as a means for building community and countering the pressures of high staff turnover and academic probation. Each year, she kept the concept of the Responsive Classroom alive in the annual school improvement plan and allocated some funds for staff training. So while Trujillo never matched Nolan in implementation of the approach, to this day the community uses Morning Meeting and other aspects of the Responsive Classroom that have been integrated into the daily routine.

Xavier South School: Little Teacher Interest, Even Less Administrative Support

Xavier South had been part of the Schools Project from the beginning. Despite many project successes, there was ongoing tension between us and many of the teachers, who believed the school's low-income African-American students needed disciplined, structured, traditional classrooms. "Responsive Classroom is too mild for these children," said a third-grade teacher. "They need firmness." These teachers considered the Responsive Classroom approach to be a mismatch for their students, and their attitudes only intensified as pressure grew to improve standardized test scores: They were fearful their students would not meet the required standards if time was taken away from core academics to promote caring and belonging. Some teachers did recognize the potential of the approach for building personal responsibility and group efficacy, but they did not see how they could take the time to implement it and at the same time meet the CPS curricular requirements. "It's bad to say that it took up too much time, because it probably would work," said one teacher, "but we have so much to do."

While the principal seemed to like the approach and encouraged teachers to implement it—he even attended the summer leadership institute in Massachusetts offered by the Northeast Foundation for Children—he did not follow through with administrative support. He was willing to spend time and money on initial training, but not to provide opportunities for ongoing professional dialogue among teachers as they implemented the approach. He gave the school's curriculum coordinator responsibility for facilitating implementation, but she had many other responsibilities that took priority. And on a more conceptual level, school administrators did not model Responsive Classroom behaviors in their interactions with teachers and students.

As a result, the Responsive Classroom was a stray at Xavier South, and implementation varied dramatically from classroom to classroom: One room would have an integrated social and academic curriculum, the day beginning with a warm and welcoming Morning Meeting, while the classroom next door would have the traditional curriculum and a teacher who could be heard yelling at students when they misbehaved. Many teachers did not want to take up the approach in full, though they were interested in adopting parts of it. "The things my students love, I keep," said one teacher, and another commented:

> By the third day, I knew I was going to commit to the Morning Meeting. I was comfortable with it, and I saw its potential for third-grade students. I was impressed with the News and Announcements letter as a way to address skill development like editing a document. . . . I also liked the fact that students were reading as soon as they walked in the room. The fact that students sat in a circle and made eye contact with one another impressed me, too.

This partial approach could work, but only if the teacher understood and bought into the overall philosophy of the Responsive Classroom. When only select components were implemented without real understanding, it appeared to us that they had less of a positive effect on children's behavior and classroom community-building.

At Xavier South, the school's collective professional capacity to create a caring, respectful environment did not change significantly, though some classrooms did reflect individual teachers' efforts to learn from their exposure to the Responsive Classroom approach.

Doyle School: An Adaptive Strategy

As at Xavier South, Doyle's student body is comprised primarily of low-income African-American children, yet the school's teachers did not consider the Responsive Classroom approach to be a cultural mismatch. Indeed, interest in the approach was high: Nearly all Doyle's staff attended the training workshop, and the curriculum coordinator and a teacher went on to attend the summer leadership institute.

Doyle's positive attitude toward the Responsive Classroom approach was influenced by the school's long, productive relationship with the Schools Project: Teachers had developed a solid knowledge base since 1989, when the partnership began, which paved the way for a real understanding of the approach; also, teachers viewed the partnership as a source of creative ideas and pedagogical support, yet they felt a sense of ownership, that decisions about how to teach ultimately rested in their hands.

This sense of ownership was strongly evidenced with the Responsive Classroom approach, as teachers adapted features to meet their needs and circumstances. Overcrowded rooms led some teachers to keep children at their desks for Morning Meeting, instead of moving them into a circle. Teachers who felt children had a hard time moving from Morning Meeting to academic lessons began to save the meeting as a reward for completed schoolwork. For older students, many teachers eliminated elements of Morning Meeting that felt too childish. Some of these adaptations were more successful than others.

Just as Doyle was beginning with the Responsive Classroom, the school was put on academic probation for low test scores. This circumstance strongly influenced teachers' feelings about using the approach:

> It's just that we have so many things to do here to get off probation. There are so many problems every morning between 8:45 and, say, 9:15 that come up. . . . I found that I needed to get to work. I found that I needed to get my reading in, and I just found that it was too difficult to do [Morning Meeting]. . . . I can see the importance of it in some ways, but I guess we're all trying so hard to bring scores up that you just feel a certain drive to get that stuff done. Even though you know these kids in particular really need a lot of counseling, loving, and all that, but you don't have the time for that because [the board of education] is holding something over your head, so you can't do that kind of stuff.

Even with this test score pressure, Doyle's teachers did not abandon the Responsive Classroom; they simply continued their adaptive strategy. Their assessments of the approach showed that they liked it overall, but they stuck with just the parts that fit easily. As one teacher put it, "Out of the teachers that I know who had the training, they liked it. We've all had problems or difficulties at one point or another and discontinued some parts of it. Like I don't use the Morning Meeting anymore. But I still use other aspects of it."

Because of this flexible attitude toward the Responsive Classroom components, the approach escaped precise definition at Doyle, though teachers universally considered it one of the school's focal points during the last years of the Schools Project.

STUDENTS, TEACHERS, SCHOOLS: THE EFFECTS OF THE RESPONSIVE CLASSROOM APPROACH

In the Schools Project, full implementation of the Responsive Classroom approach was rare, yet even partial implementation yielded meaningful effects on students, teachers, and schools as a whole. Teachers did not have to take up all the components to start to see changes in themselves and their students, and schools did not have to mandate full participation to start to look and feel different.

Changes in Students

The component of the Responsive Classroom approach that was adopted most widely in the partner schools was Morning Meeting, and students universally loved it. They delighted in coming together in an informal manner at the start of each day. "We have fun at the meetings, we laugh. It's like jokes," a third-grade student said. Teachers, too, noted the positive effects of Morning Meeting. "I like the fact that it's given a different structure to the day," commented one teacher. "I like the fact that the kids feel that sense that they are part of a group. They fix each other. They are a unit. They care about each other."

Morning Meeting provided an opportunity for students to learn about one another and become more empathic. A second-grade student at Nolan School, for example, developed diabetes and had to keep an insulin kit at school for emergencies. Her classmates' frequent questions about her illness began to bother her. She asked her teacher if she could use Morning Meeting to explain her diabetes to the other students and show them her insulin kit. Her sharing during the meeting enabled her to communicate important information about herself, and it gave her classmates a chance to communicate understanding and respect.

In some classrooms, the sense of community engendered by Morning Meeting spilled over into the rest of the day. "There is no bickering in our classroom," said a child. "Students in our room stick around each other." In these classrooms, Rules and Logical Consequences often served as an ongoing reminder and reaffirmation of the desired social behaviors. As one student related, "The rules help us remember to treat others as we would like to be treated. We don't harm each other." In a similar vein, a student from another school said, "One of our rules is to be friends, to treat others like you want to be treated. This means we can't leave anyone out or say things to hurt other people's feelings."

Children's actions showed that they were internalizing the Responsive Classroom philosophy and accepting responsibility for their role as a member of a caring learning community. One morning, a Nolan student was crying inconsolably over a family problem. Three classmates asked the teacher if they could talk to the distraught student. One explained earnestly, "Remember when I shared? I talked about that very same problem. I know how she feels." The four children were allowed to go out into the hall to talk privately; within 10 minutes they reentered the classroom, the troubled student comforted and ready to settle into the school day.

As children's behavior improved and their sense of belonging grew, their capacity for learning increased. As one teacher explained:

> A lot of the teachers came to visit my room to see how it works, and a lot of people said that my classroom was one of the better-behaved classrooms because of what I attribute to the Responsive Classroom. Getting to know each other better, working on social skills, kind of helped to improve the behavior in my classroom. And, of course, when you can improve behavior, you can finally get to teach.

Teachers also felt that the approach contributed in more direct ways to children's cognitive development. Morning Meeting activities, for example, were often credited with improving students' reading and oral skills: "The students absolutely love it. They come together. They learn speaking skills. They learn to focus on the speaker, to have eye contact, to ask questions. It's genuine. It's a real-life situation where they have to use communication skills."

There was one more effect of the Responsive Classroom on students that was especially gratifying to teachers: Many children began to develop a love for school. A third-grader at Xavier South exclaimed, "I think my classroom is happy! People are smiling every time they come into the classroom, because they are happy to come to school."

Changes in Teachers

Teachers in the partner schools fell into three groups in regard to the Responsive Classroom approach. For the first group, the approach represented a philosophy that could encompass everything from community-building to curricular development. These teachers had a deeper understanding of the principles of the Responsive Classroom, and they were able to wholly incorporate it into their classrooms and adapt components as needed.

The second group understood the Responsive Classroom as a toolbox of techniques, particularly in regard to behavior management. They generally had little understanding of the approach's theoretical framework and implemented activities in a prescriptive, superficial manner, though even at this level the approach had noticeable effects, and the teachers valued it.

Finally, some teachers considered the Responsive Classroom to be the brainchild of educators who did not understand the needs of children in disadvantaged communities. These teachers believed that their students needed tight structure and punitive discipline to achieve. While there was at least one teacher in each partner school who held this opinion, in two schools a large number of teachers considered the approach to be inappropriate for their students.

Throughout the years of the Schools Project, we had encountered such diverse views among teachers—in fact, we expected to encounter them. Following the principles of the enabling approach, we had always made a point of trying to cultivate teacher buy-in for interventions by providing opportunities for them to explore the consonance and dissonance among the tenets of the intervention, their own beliefs about teaching and learning, and the realities of their professional situations. Through this process, teachers were often able to move closer to a shared vision and find at least some elements of value in the intervention for their own classrooms. The process also established personal connections between teachers and us and provided us with valuable information about their work settings, instructional skills, and attitudes toward professional change, which enabled us to customize interventions.

Unfortunately, the training model used by the Northeast Foundation for Children did not follow the same approach as the Schools Project. It offered a set of preestablished tools for building a caring school community, assuming that the workshop participants were already philosophically aligned with the principles of the Responsive Classroom. While true for some participants, it was not the case for all, and the training did not provide extensive enough opportunities for the kind of in-depth conversation and reflection necessary for teachers to modify their beliefs and attitudes.

Just how problematic this could be became evident when teachers returned to their classrooms and began to implement the approach. As some of them struggled with implementation, the value of the enabling approach—the co-construction of goals and strategies—became clear to both us and teachers. Neglecting this process lessened the effects of the Responsive Classroom in many cases. It also colored the view of the partnership for schools that did not have prior experience with the Schools Project: Many teachers in these schools saw us only as advocates of a single strategy, instead of as facilitators of problem-solving around a particular issue.

In retrospect, we realized we should have augmented the foundation's training or preceded it with the type of reading and discussion period we had organized at Nolan School. Nolan was the only partner school where teachers had the opportunity to critically explore the philosophy of the Responsive Classroom in relation to their own values, practices, and school setting. And in the end, Nolan was the only partner school where the approach really took root and flourished.

Whether converts or dissenters, however, all teachers in the partner schools recited the same litany of implementation difficulties regarding the Responsive Classroom: large class sizes, limited classroom space, and not enough time in the day. For some teachers, these challenges were a justification for rejecting the Responsive Classroom approach; for others, though, they were the impetus for generating a stronger commitment to the approach, for assuming ownership and finding ways to make it work.

Changes in Schools

For whole schools to become caring, respectful communities, administrative leadership and support are essential. It is not enough, however, for administrators to verbally endorse the approach, or attend a summer leadership institute, or even mandate that teachers implement the approach. Administrators did these things in nearly all the partner schools, yet in most of the schools change was limited to particular classrooms and did not extend to the community at large.

At Nolan School, which was completely transformed by the Responsive Classroom approach, administrative leadership and support were manifest at many different levels, from paying stipends to teachers for time spent learning about and discussing the approach, to reorganizing the daily schedule so that everyone would participate in Morning Meeting, to modeling the principles of the approach in interactions with staff and students. Nolan's administration helped the entire school community, including parents, acquire a shared understanding of the philosophy and purposes of the Responsive Classroom, and the administration also embraced schoolwide rituals that sustained and celebrated the school as a caring, respectful learning community that values all its members.

Nolan represents the potential of urban schools. It stands in stark contrast to the highly publicized images of disorderly classrooms, helpless teachers, frustrated administrators, and disinterested parents. While everyone in the Nolan community deserves credit for the changes the school underwent, the depth and breadth of change would not have been possible without the active and sensitive participation of the administration.

CHAPTER 7

Brave New World

Computers in the Classroom

ONE OF THE MOST SIGNIFICANT CHANGES in Chicago's schools over the past 15 years has been the role of computer technology. When the Schools Project began in 1987, few school administrators in the city were interested in investing scarce resources in technology, and just as few teachers were interested in learning how to integrate technology into the classroom. During the first phase of the project, computer technology was not even considered as an area of intervention.

The situation changed rather quickly, however, and by the early 1990s, all the partner schools had a computer lab, and some teachers in every school were interested in exploring technology's potential. When working in the partner schools in other areas, more and more frequently we received questions from teachers about hardware and software. Unfortunately, none of the project staff at the time had much expertise in that area, but as it became clear to us that the schools' technology needs were only going to increase, we hired a new staff member, Elizabeth Beyer, to integrate technology into the ongoing work of the project.

WHERE TO START?

Energetic and eager, Elizabeth began traveling from school to school as soon as she joined the team, talking with administrators, teachers, and computer coordinators. Very soon she realized that the technology needs of the partner schools were not only diverse, but vague, as few schools could clearly identify their priorities. Determining priorities was essentially a catch-22: Administrators didn't want to spend money on classroom computers because teachers didn't know how to use the technology, but teachers couldn't learn to use the technology if they didn't have computers in the classroom.

To help schools figure out where they were and where they wanted to go with technology, Elizabeth developed the Five-A framework, which she adapted from the Apple Classrooms of Tomorrow Project (Baker, Herman, & Gearhat, 1989; Dwyer, Ringstaff, & Sandholtz, 1991; Sandholtz, Ringstaff, & Dwyer, 1997). Within her framework, there are five developmental stages of technology use in the classroom:

1. *Anticipation*—There may be a computer lab in the school, but there are not yet computers in classrooms. Some teachers are resistant to the idea of technology, and even those who are excited about it feel anxious, because they lack computer skills.
2. *Arrival*—There are now computers in classrooms and teachers are learning to operate them, but they still feel a great deal of anxiety about technology and do not yet use it for educational activities.
3. *Automation*—Teachers begin to use technology to automate educational activities that are already part of the normal classroom environment.
4. *Adaptation*—Teachers begin to use technology to extend and expand educational activities, creating new avenues for teaching and learning.
5. *Appropriation*—Technology is fully integrated into the classroom, as teachers regularly and purposefully use it to enhance curriculum, instruction, and assessment.

For each stage, Elizabeth developed a list of learning goals for students, teachers, and parents, including specific activities to reach each goal. (The Five-A framework is described in detail in Beyer, 1994.)

When Elizabeth started working with the partner schools, they were all in the Anticipation stage. Elizabeth wrote of her first visit to Nolan School (Beyer, 1997):

> The principal, supportive of the idea of using computers, was the first to introduce me to the computer lab. Before we could get into the lab on the second floor of the building, we had to unlock the huge padlock on a metal gate that extended across the regular door to the computer lab. The principal explained that this metal gate was the best part of the computer lab because it prevented computer theft: "No computer has ever been stolen from our school," he boasted.
>
> The lab in 1992 had approximately 25 Apple IIe computers. The computer teacher, although computer literate and open to learning, was officially a teacher's aide. The plan for computer instruction was that children of all grades visited the lab once a week. They shared computers and played some drill and practice programs. There was no communication between the com-

puter teacher and classroom teachers, and not a single classroom had a computer. Although three computers were on carts and could be rolled among
classrooms, [school] rules prohibited this. (p. 3)

In reality, *alienation* might have been a better word to describe Nolan's stage
of technology development.

Once a school begins to install computers in classrooms, teacher training is the key to moving through the developmental stages of the Five-A
model. When technology is used without adequate training and support,
it can disrupt classrooms' existing social organization, threaten teachers'
sense of competence and authority, and interfere with teaching and learning processes (O'Neil, 2000; Schofield, 1995; Siegel, 1995; Technology
Counts, 1999).

Training by the Schools Project occurred at vastly different rates in the
partner schools, depending on the level of administrative support and
participation; teachers' level of interest and motivation; the presence of a
computer coordinator; and the level of resources allocated for technology.
As was common practice during the Schools Project, teacher participation
in training was voluntary, though in some schools administrators would
not allow teachers to get a computer in their classroom unless they participated in training.

Training consisted of both group courses and individual, classroom-
based support. Most teachers needed to start with the basics, such as boot-
ing up and learning to use the keyboard and mouse. In the beginning, the
training participants were usually tense and apprehensive. One teacher
described her first experience with a computer in her classroom right after
beginning training:

> I rolled a computer into my room after the lunch break. All 30 children
> thronged around to see what it would do, but I could not find the switch
> to turn it on. I was flustered and yelled at the children, "You all sit down
> until I turn the computer on!" Jonathan volunteered to help me. And I
> said, "No, not now!" I did find the switch after a complete body search
> of the computer, but nothing happened when I turned it on. Finally, I
> had to ask for Jonathan's help, and it turned out I had not plugged it in.
> This is probably one of the most embarrassing moments in my life.

Another teacher, commenting on the progress of technology at her school,
put it well:

> You know, many of our students are not using computers for learning
> yet, because I don't think some teachers are very comfortable with it

themselves. They're real afraid of the students knowing more than they know on the computer. They don't want to look like they don't know what they're talking about.

Clearly, it was going to be a long road to Appropriation.

KEY FEATURES OF TEACHER TRAINING IN TECHNOLOGY

Through the Schools Project, as well as other Erikson Institute initiatives since then, we have learned many lessons about how to conduct teacher training in technology. All of these lessons can be applied to teachers' professional development in other areas, although they are particularly important in regard to technology training, which presents some unique challenges (Hawkins, Spielvogel, & Panush, 1996; Honey, Culp, & Carrigg, 2000). These challenges reflect teachers' generally low level of technology preparedness, as well as the nature of computer technology itself, with its ever-extendable capacities and ever-changing functions.

Allow Time to Learn, Practice, and Develop

In most schools, computer training consists of a "one-shot" workshop, usually no more than a day or two long (CEO Forum on Education and Technology, 1997; Conte, 1997). Based on our experience and the literature in the field, we do not recommend such brief, condensed training, as it does not allow sufficient time to acquire and master new skills and ideas (Garet, Porter, Desimone, Birman, & Yoon, 2001; McGillivray, 2000). Unfortunately, in some of the partner schools, limited resources and interest dictated that we provide this type of training. In a couple of the schools, however, we were able to conduct a 10-week, 30-hour course, which allowed us to relay a small amount of information at each session and to ensure that participants fully understood it before moving on to the next skill or idea. Also, between sessions, participants could apply what they had learned in their own classrooms and then bring questions back to the training instructor at the next session.

Commenting on her "distributed learning" experience, one Schools Project teacher said:

In my 30 years of teaching, I participated in many professional development activities, but computer learning presented a host of different challenges. Every time I was with the computer instructor, I felt okay

with what I learned. When I came back to my own classroom, everything I learned turned against me . . . the computer layout was different, I
wasn't able to do the same thing as in the training session anymore, etc.
Fortunately, I could come back again and again to ask the instructor. If
not for this kind of training, I am sure I would not feel as comfortable
with the computer as I do now.

In technology training courses developed by Erikson since the Schools
Project, the duration of the course has actually been increased. Trainers
have found that 15 to 20 hours is ideal for a single topic, whether the topic
is computer basics, selection and integration of children's software, or creation of instructional materials with a computer.

Bridge Known Content to New Content

For teachers unaccustomed to technology, a computer can be very threatening. Even today in our technology training courses, we find many teachers for whom the computer is not a natural part of the home or work
environment. We have found that an effective way to reduce teachers'
initial computer anxiety is to have them explore children's software programs. Whether the content of the software is language, math, science, or
social studies, it is within teachers' existing knowledge base, which engen-
ders a sense of security for them. Describing her initial training experience,
one teacher said:

> I knew almost nothing when I started the training, and I was so scared
> to even touch a computer. But when I saw other teachers play *Dr.
> Seuss Preschool* [a children's software program], I got so interested in it
> that I started following them and played for more than an hour. I
> totally forgot about how little I knew about the computer—I simply
> enjoyed too much that *Dr. Seuss*.

This method of training does not disregard the importance of acquiring knowledge of computer basics. Rather, it presents an alternate route
to acquisition: As teachers explore children's software, we introduce computer basics at appropriate points within the context of the exploration.
By creating a bridge from known to new content, learning becomes
less threatening and more meaningful (Rogoff, 1990; Tharp & Gallimore,
1995). This method of training also helps teachers become familiar with
children's software programs and begin to think of how to use them in
the classroom.

Foster Active Learning

Active learning is the process by which an individual, whether a child or an adult, participates in the construction of knowledge by interacting with the environment and other people. Active as opposed to passive learning is generally considered to lead to fuller understanding and a greater capacity to use the knowledge (Bransford, Brown, & Cocking, 1999; Piaget, 1985; Vygotsky, 1986).

There are several ways that we foster active learning among teachers in technology training. First and most obvious, hands-on computer experience is central to the training: No one can master hardware or software without actually using them, and mastery usually requires repeated practice.

Another key to active learning is to encourage participation in the development of the training, which can be accomplished through a range of strategies. In our training, for example, instructors always prepare and present an outline at the beginning of the course, but they also allow participants to help determine the content and format of the training over time. When a participant brings feedback or a question to the instructor, for instance, it is usually incorporated into the training. Also, many handouts are developed with participants' input, and as participants discover or develop technology strategies, tricks, and shortcuts, they are asked to share them with the entire class.

Another way to encourage participation is to have the more technologically adept participants serve as assistant teachers or mentors, since the best way to internalize a concept or skill is to teach it to someone else (Bransford, Brown, & Cocking, 1999). This strategy is also very helpful to the instructor when the class is large and individualized attention is difficult to provide.

Promote Collective Training Experiences

Individual classroom-based support is a critical aspect of technology training, but collective training experiences contribute in important ways to the process, by allowing for collaborative learning, fostering collegiality, and even speeding up skill acquisition and mastery (Downes, Arthur, & Beecher, 2001; International Society for Technology in Education, 2002; McGillivray, 2000). By *collective training,* we mean training offered to a group of teachers from the same grade level and/or the same school. There are several advantages to this approach when it comes to computer training. First, it helps reduce some teachers' anxiety about technology when familiar colleagues are going through the training alongside them. Second, when trainees share curriculum goals, or work within the same technology constraints, or have other grade-level or school conditions in common, their computer training can be more targeted, addressing the concerns and issues particular to the group. Also, when teachers are from the same school, it is easier for them to share software or create multimedia projects together outside training, opening doors for further collaboration and development of a shared professional culture.

We have found that in the case of technology training, it is important for teachers and their classroom assistants to participate together. In early childhood classrooms in particular, it is usual to have a teacher and an assistant, but the common practice in regard to most types of professional development is for only the teacher to participate. It is very important that young children always be supervised and guided while working at the computer, however, and when both teacher and assistant are trained in technology, it means that there can always be a technologically competent adult in the classroom's computer center. Further, the two can support each other in integrating technology into the learning process. We have also seen many classrooms where the assistant takes on primary responsibility for the computer center, thereby freeing the teacher for other activities.

BUILDING SITE-BASED TECHNOLOGY LEADERSHIP AND EXPERTISE

Even though we were willing to provide ongoing technology support as part of the Schools Project, there were not enough of us to meet the partner schools' needs. To increase the likelihood of the effective use of computer technology in the classroom, it was necessary to develop site-based leadership and expertise (Filer, Heritage, & Gallimore, 2000; Honey & Henriquez, 1996). Furthermore, developing site-based leadership and expertise was in keeping with the principles of the enabling approach.

Jie-Qi Chen, Julie Walstra, and Warren Dym, the three project staff members who took primary responsibility for technology activities when Elizabeth Beyer left the project, together designed an intimate 9-month seminar to develop technology leaders in the partner schools. The seminar met every 2 weeks, 3 hours each time, at Erikson Institute. Teachers, curriculum coordinators, and technology coordinators from the partner schools were all invited, but because of the time commitment and the content of the training, only five people—one from each school in the project at the time—attended the seminar in its entirety: four technology coordinators and one technology-minded, motivated teacher who served as the unofficial coordinator at her school.

The leadership seminar was designed around four core principles: knowledge, practice, reflection, and relationship. Like the training best practices outlined earlier in the chapter, these principles can be applied to leadership development in any pedagogical area, though they take on a particular shape in the context of technology.

Knowledge: Establishing an Advanced Knowledge Base

Interestingly enough, none of the five coordinators had any formal training in instructional technology or a related field, so one of the first goals of the seminar was to fill in any gaps in technology knowledge and skills, to ensure a strong foundation for other seminar activities and for leadership at school. Julie, an experienced school technology coordinator, served as the seminar instructor. Among the many topics she covered, the following were considered the most useful by the seminar participants:

- Understanding the Windows and Macintosh operating systems, including tips on how to make the systems "behave" and descriptions of the similarities and differences between the two systems.
- Mastering a variety of standard software packages, such as ClarisWorks, PowerPoint, and Excel, in order to use a computer to create presentations, spreadsheets, charts and tables, newsletters, and classroom layouts.
- Designing and managing a computer lab, including how to set up the lab to suit children of different ages and how to create a file locking system to protect files from accidental modification or deletion.
- Developing computer-based tools for classroom management, in order to facilitate such daily tasks as student sign-in, lunch counts, and the tracking of student progress.
- Reviewing different types of children's software and learning how to evaluate the programs and integrate them into the teaching and learning process.

The content of the sessions on these topics was not derived from published books or manuals, but from Julie's years of experience in the field and from the needs and concerns presented by the participants themselves.

Practice: Practicing Leadership Skills in the School Setting

Because the seminar lasted an entire school year, participants had the opportunity to act as leaders in their schools while still receiving support and guidance from Julie, Jie-Qi, and Warren and from other seminar participants. The seminar itself provided two important avenues for practicing leadership skills in the school setting: the development and implementation of school-based technology training programs and the creation of school technology plans.

The technology coordinators knew they would be expected to provide individual, classroom-based support to teachers at their schools, but we also wanted them to be able to provide formal group training experiences. Thus, a core activity for participants during the seminar was to develop and implement a school-based technology training program. Jie-Qi and Warren first assisted the coordinators in conducting a needs assessment at their school. The coordinators then brought the results to the seminar, to analyze and use them as a basis for designing site-based training programs. The content of the programs ended up varying from school to school, as did the duration of the training and the time it was offered—during preparation periods, after school, or on professional development days.

During the school year, the technology coordinators offered and led a total of 50 training sessions in their schools, each lasting about 2 hours, in which approximately 100 teachers and parents participated. The coordinators were proud of the training they provided—"Teachers, parents, and career service aides showed genuine interest . . . and got something out of the class," said one—and they also felt that designing and conducting the training increased their own technology knowledge and skills. One of the coordinators commented, "Each time you get on the computer, you learn something different or new that you didn't know before."

Also during the school year, all public schools in Chicago for the first time were required to write an annual technology plan. The partner schools' administrators turned this responsibility over to the seminar participants. We gave them sample technology plans to review and carefully went over with them the instructions regarding the content and structure of the plans they were to submit. In preparing the plans, the coordinators exchanged ideas and critiqued one another's drafts. All but one of the technology plans were approved by the Illinois Board of Education on the first submission, a real accomplishment for these technologically nascent schools. One seminar participant said, "Without Erikson, without everybody else's help, this task would not have been possible for me."

Reflection: Becoming a More Effective Leader Through Reflection

We built in regular opportunities for reflection during the seminar, since reflection helps people distill meaning from their experiences (Costa & Kallick, 2000). During each session, we set aside approximately 30 minutes for reflection. Sometimes we would propose a topic for discussion among the participants, while other times group members were encouraged to bring up whatever was on their minds that was related to school technology development.

On a practical level, we promoted reflection on pedagogical, methodological, and logistical issues that arose during the year, in order to help the coordinators achieve ever-higher levels of mastery. For example, when the coordinators taught their newly developed school-based computer training courses, we conducted observations. Back in the seminar, we used the observations as a springboard for group discussions, and over the course of the school year, the coordinators' training programs improved noticeably.

We also encouraged reflection on a personal level by asking the participants to consider such questions as "What are my beliefs and values as a computer educator?" and "What are my strengths and weaknesses as a computer educator?" Such lines of reflection proved critical to the leadership development of the participants. When Mrs. Oaks, Doyle's coordinator, first learned she would have to teach a technology training course for teachers at her school, for example, she was overwhelmed by fear and anxiety: "I can't do it!" "I'm not good enough!" "I can't teach male teachers!" As she discussed her worries, it became apparent that her personal history as both a woman and an African American had contributed to her sense of inadequacy in the realm of technology. By posing a few key questions—for example, "What is good enough?" "Can we learn to be good enough?" "Are there negative stereotypes of minority women in the fields of science and technology?" "Besides being victims of these stereotypes, do we contribute to them?"—Jie-Qi led a group discussion during which all the seminar participants expressed strong feelings. In the end, everyone benefited from the discussion, but especially Mrs. Oaks, who realized she *could* teach the technology training course. The group also came away from the discussion more sensitive to the technology-related insecurities that might plague others in their schools, whether teachers, students, or parents.

Relationship: Building Relationships to Create
a Leadership-Support Network

Coming into the leadership seminar, all of the participants felt isolated. Lamented one technology coordinator, "I have no one to talk to about my problems and struggles. No one has the time or interest to listen to me." The discussion and reflection time built into each seminar session, as well as the collaborative activities during the sessions, served not only to promote individual leadership development, but also to establish a network of trusting relationships with peers that could provide ongoing professional and personal support. The participants all valued the network that developed through the seminar, which helped them feel they were "not alone in [their] struggle to push technology at school." One coordinator said, "This is the one place where I come and learn that other people have similar problems. . . . I don't feel so isolated anymore, because I know there are people standing behind me when I have problems. It makes us a strong group."

Because of the strong relationships that developed within the seminar, the participants began to collaborate frequently outside of it, visiting one another's schools to help upgrade computer labs and troubleshoot, for example, and e-mailing technology questions back and forth. This network of support contributed to each technology coordinator's effectiveness at work, ongoing professional development, and emotional stability.

THE DIVERSE ROLES OF TECHNOLOGY COORDINATORS

There were commonalities in how the five technology coordinators from the seminar fulfilled their role back in their home schools—for example, they all provided both group training experiences and individualized support, and they all wrote school technology plans—but differences emerged over time, the result of variation among the schools and also among the coordinators themselves. In this section, we highlight some of the diverse activities in which the coordinators were involved; while none of the coordinators would be comfortable claiming full credit for these achievements, they certainly played a vital role in them.

Doyle School

As a school on academic probation, Doyle's primary goal was to improve students' reading scores. In response to this pressure, Mrs. Oaks, the school's technology coordinator, looked for ways to use computers to facilitate students' acquisition and mastery of reading skills. For example, she purchased a number of educational software programs focused on basic reading skills and reading comprehension; teachers could borrow them for classroom use, and children could use them in the afterschool program as well. She also downloaded short e-books from the Internet and distributed them to classrooms as additional reading material. For teachers comfortable with technology, Mrs. Oaks's efforts were a useful supplement to the regular reading program.

Xavier South School

Xavier decided that even the youngest students should be introduced to computers and scheduled all kindergartners and first-graders for the computer lab 4 days a week, half an hour each day. To accommodate these young learners, Mr. Hanks, the technology coordinator, set up four different stations in the lab, which made use not only of computers but of audiotapes, books, and art materials as well: There was a computer station, a journal station, a writing and typing station, and a listening station. Every few weeks, Mr. Hanks, in consultation with classroom teachers, would put together a new set of games and activities for each station, often with a common theme, and children would work together in groups to complete them. For example, children might listen to a story at the listening station. They could then use a software program based on the same story at the computer station. Next they could draw pictures based on the story at the journal station. And finally, at the writing and typing station, they could type and edit their own version of the story on a computer using the KidPix program. By setting up the computer lab this way for the young children, Mr. Hanks demonstrated how technology can be integrated with more traditional classroom activities, instead of used in isolation.

Nathan School

At Nathan, there was no official technology coordinator position at the time. Ms. Anderson, the seminar participant from the school, was a regular classroom teacher interested in technology: Whatever she did to promote technology development at Nathan was done on her own time and with little administrative support.

The size and layout of Nathan made her work even harder: At the time, Nathan had about 1,000 students and 60 teachers divided among three locations in the neighborhood because of a lack of space. The school had no computer lab, though many classrooms had computers. Some were not even plugged in, however, and others had simply been pushed out into the hallway, because, as one teacher said, "[They're] of no use for me, and my room was packed already."

Despite all these obstacles, Ms. Anderson managed to train half of the school's teachers in group sessions and dramatically increased the use of technology in the classroom. All trained teachers, for example, began using computers to create parent newsletters and student worksheets. Some of them also learned to download information from the Internet for curriculum projects. Children in these classrooms started to use computers to explore educational software and work on multimedia projects. These activities may not sound very impressive to someone who is technologically savvy, but at Nathan, where so many teachers did not even know how to use a keyboard or move a mouse at the beginning of computer training, these were significant achievements.

As the unofficial technology coordinator, Ms. Anderson accomplished a huge amount, but we would not recommend that schools follow this approach. Instead, schools should create and fully support a position whose sole responsibility is to lead and coordinate technology-related activities in the school.

Nolan School

Mrs. Larson, a teacher's aide, also served as technology coordinator at Nolan. In addition to assisting individual teachers in their use of computer technology, she helped to install an accelerated-reader software program in all the classrooms. Students could check out accelerated-reader books from the classroom. When they'd finished a book, they could log onto the computer in the classroom and answer a series of questions about it, and the computer would keep a record of students' answers, including the percentage of correct ones. This reading program was not viewed as a substitute for teacher-led reading instruction, but as a valuable tool for getting children interested in reading and for compiling useful information about their reading progress.

With Mrs. Larson's guidance, Nolan also applied for and received a grant that allowed the school to install a T-line connection for fast data transmission, to network the school's computers, and to establish an interactive relationship with a Chicago museum. Teachers and museum educators would communicate through e-mail and a chat room about ways to use museum resources for studying different subject areas and creating integrated projects.

Trujillo School

Among the seminar participants, Mr. Sanchez, Trujillo's technology coordinator, had the broadest view of what his role could be: He envisioned technology as a means to transform and bind the whole school community—not only teachers and students, but parents and others in the neighborhood as well.

Like Doyle, Trujillo was on academic probation, so the school was focused on improving reading scores. Trujillo's challenges were even greater, however, since it is a bilingual school whose students need to learn to read in both English and Spanish. The school had few printed books in both languages, so Mr. Sanchez purchased software containing bilingual texts; using an LCD panel, the texts could be projected onto the wall, large enough for all the children in the classroom to follow.

Mr. Sanchez also spearheaded the opening of a computer club at a local mental health center that was intended as a place for children to go after school to gain experience with various software programs and the Internet and to get help with homework. To support the club, Mr. Sanchez sought financial assistance from a range of sources, including local businesses: He went from store to store in the neighborhood, chatting with owners about the importance of such a club for disadvantaged children and helping the owners recognize that the club would also mean less loitering outside their shops after school. Through these efforts, the club became a joint project between Trujillo and a host of community institutions.

Mr. Sanchez also developed a course for Trujillo parents to simultaneously learn English and word-processing skills, both of which are important for getting good-paying jobs. Having worked in Hispanic communities for years, he had heard innumerable stories about missed employment opportunities because of limited English or a lack of basic computer skills.

A unique feature of the parent computer course was devised by Mr. Sanchez in collaboration with Trujillo's parent council. The course—scheduled for 6 weeks, 3 hours a week—was free. For each hour of instruction, however, parents were expected to volunteer 1 hour at school, using their newly acquired computer knowledge and skills to assist the technology coordinator and the teachers. This arrangement created a mutually beneficial relationship between parents and the school: Each had something to offer the other, and there was a fair exchange of time and talent.

At the end of the year, 32 parents had completed the 18-hour course and received a certificate, and Mr. Sanchez himself was given a trophy by Trujillo for his efforts to advance technology in the school and to create a bridge between the school and the community.

Nowadays, nearly all public schools in the United States are reported to have computer access within the school building, and the *concept* of computer technology, at least, is no longer novel to teachers (Technology Counts, 1999, 2002). What hasn't changed since the early years of the Schools Project, however, is the need for teacher training and support in the field of technology (Honey, Culp, & Carrigg, 2000; Panel on Educational Technology, 1997). The ways that computers are used for educational purposes vary drastically from state to state, district to district, school to school, and even classroom to classroom (Becker, 2000; Technology Counts, 2001).

Given the continuing high interest in the role of technology in education, it would seem to be an area of real potential for university–school partnerships, one that is even attractive to funders. As the Schools Project experience highlights, the most critical piece of technology development in schools—the piece a university–school partnership might focus on—is the establishment of site-based leadership and expertise. By building this role into the school structure, teacher training and support can be more customized, flexible, prompt, and affordable than if leadership and expertise reside on the university side. Even after the partnership ends, the school will be able to continue its technology development on its own, particularly if the position of technology coordinator is fully supported by school administrators and is part of a network of coordinators in the district.

PART III

Lessons from More Than a Decade of Partnership

CHAPTER 8

The Teachers' Perspective

Findings from the Schools Project Evaluation

THE THIRD-PARTY EVALUATION of the Schools Project took place in 1998, as the initiative was drawing to a close. For the evaluation, Erikson Institute contracted with Ruanda Garth McCullough and Karen DeMoss of the Consortium on Chicago School Research at the University of Chicago, both experienced researchers with a deep understanding of the history of Chicago school reform. Their charge was to answer three general questions:

1. What effects did the Schools Project have on practices in the partner schools?
2. How did teachers respond to Erikson's partnering approach?
3. Which changes in the schools did teachers attribute to the Schools Project?

The evaluation was conducted in the five schools that were still in the project at that time: Doyle, Nathan, Nolan, Trujillo, and Xavier South. Over the course of 6 months, Ruanda and Karen conducted an all-staff survey, interviewed a sample of personnel at each school, conducted random classroom observations, and attended a variety of school events. Using data from these activities, they wrote a case study of each school and compiled the survey responses (see Appendix C for summaries of the survey results). Additionally, they conducted interviews with staff at Ivy and Wheaton, which had left the Schools Project earlier, in order to examine whether project effects were sustained beyond the life of the partnership.

Across the five primary evaluation schools, the survey revealed general satisfaction with the partnerships:

- A majority of teachers felt the Schools Project effectively addressed the needs of their school, classroom, and students.
- A majority of teachers felt they changed positively through their partnership experience; in particular, their motivation to improve as teachers had increased, though they also felt that their pedagogical knowledge, repertoire of instructional techniques, and access to materials had all increased through the partnership.
- Nearly half the teachers believed that the Schools Project had been instrumental in bringing about whole-school change.

While it was rewarding to learn that in the schools the overall view of the project was positive, we knew that the survey findings masked a diversity of experiences, which were revealed by the evaluators in the individual school case studies. From the case studies, five themes emerged that recurred across the schools, reflecting a more complex and realistic view of the partnering process than the survey results alone communicate:

1. Erikson's partnership approach was as important as any particular intervention to teachers and proved to be one of the most enduring aspects of the Schools Project.
2. Teachers wanted more from us—more training opportunities, more one-on-one consultations, and more exposure to other teachers successfully meeting the challenges of working in low-income urban schools.
3. Administrative attitudes and actions strongly affected the degree to which project efforts became part of the fabric of a school.
4. Whole-school change could also be thwarted by other factors working alone or in concert, including ideological and racial differences between school and project staff.
5. At an individual level, many teachers changed dramatically, and the changes were lasting, even when whole-school change did not occur.

In earlier chapters of this book, we touched on all these themes, particularly as they related to specific areas of intervention, such as developmentally appropriate practice, the Responsive Classroom approach, or technology integration. In this chapter, we examine the themes independent of specific interventions, as important lessons from the Schools Project in and of themselves.

THE ENABLING APPROACH: IN TEACHERS' EYES,
A MODEL FOR PARTNERING

Chicago schools are blessed—or cursed, depending on the vantage point—with a host of nearby universities and philanthropic organizations interested in public education. Since the 1988 Chicago school reforms, researchers and reformers have become such a part of the daily landscape of city schools that, as Ruanda noted, getting access to conduct evaluations is sometimes difficult, because school staff understandably have "researcher fatigue." In the case of the Schools Project evaluation, however, in every partner school but one—Xavier South (discussed below)—Ruanda and Karen encountered no obstacles. Both researchers had considerable experience negotiating smooth entries into schools, but they attributed their warm reception in large part to teachers' positive experiences during the project, stemming from Erikson's approach to partnering.

We had never laid out the specifics of the enabling approach in talking with teachers or administrators, and neither did Ruanda or Karen. Yet in the course of the evaluation, teachers spoke of the project in terms that validated each of the three principles of the enabling approach:

1. A preconceived educational program brought in from outside needs to be adapted to the circumstances of individual schools and teachers.
2. Teachers' engagement and support are more likely to occur when they play an active role in identifying needs and developing goals.
3. The quality of the relationship between a school and the "enabling" partner is directly related to the quality of school growth and change that occurs.

Teachers recognized the degree to which we tailored interventions and technical assistance, not only for each school but for individual teachers within the school. Teachers repeatedly told Ruanda and Karen that project staff were "very flexible," and many spoke about how they had been encouraged to adapt what they learned and to apply what was most appropriate: "I just feel comfortable with [the initiative] because I can do my own thing," said one teacher. "Do my own thing," of course, does not mean that the Schools Project had no expectations or standards, but how they were applied varied according to a teacher's levels of experience and expertise, as well as other factors. Teachers frequently noted that they were able to build on their own styles and strengths:

You know how our personalities are part of us, and so when Renee first came, I would tell her, "I'm kind of a pack rat." People can be very possessive, but they were able to help me get rid of things. She was able to work with me in such a way that I was able to welcome her help. . . . We can help ourselves in changing our patterns with the kind of help that is a help instead of the kind that condemns.

Among teachers in the evaluation, gratitude for receiving "help that is a help" was repeated time and again.

In preparing the case studies, Ruanda and Karen commented to us that there was so much variation across the five schools in the types of assistance received, they had trouble producing an evaluation product for Erikson that preserved the integrity of the experiences at each school and also provided a comparable view of the Schools Project from site to site. The variation across schools was the result not only of customization, but of responsiveness to teachers' specific requests and interests as well. Teachers in the evaluation consistently remarked on the degree to which their input was solicited and incorporated in the partnership process. There were, of course, big issues, such as teachers' concerns about children's behavior in the classroom or raising reading scores and getting off probation; these concerns prompted us to move the partnerships in new directions. But in the evaluation, it was the little acts of responsiveness to their requests that teachers remembered most: our gathering samples of curricula, assessment forms, and instructional materials; arranging visits to other schools; locating research articles; planning field trips and school celebrations; just listening when teachers needed to vent. One teacher commented, "They would come in and even rearrange your room if you asked," and another said, "I just never met anybody who was so responsive to the kinds of things that we needed."

Many teachers in the evaluation commented on the quality of their relationships with project staff. Ruanda and Karen noted that at the beginning of interviews, when they explained the confidentiality of the evaluation to teachers, many were quick to make such comments as "Oh, I don't have anything bad to say about Erikson," or "Patty's been great," or "Renee is a fine person." Many teachers echoed the opinion of a teacher who talked about the importance of the individuals partnering with the school:

They are people that could really work with us as we are. I think that Erikson did a really good job in selecting people who could work with us. . . . I developed a rapport with them, and I think that was very, very good. Now perhaps someone different might not have worked as well, so I think that [the choice of individuals] is very important.

In the evaluation, teachers overwhelmingly shared the feeling that we respected them as professionals, treating them as capable while at the same time creating opportunities for them to improve. The interviews suggested that teachers knew they were respected because they were not put down or judged. Karen and Ruanda noted that teachers in urban school systems rarely receive thanks or praise for their efforts, and our doing so encouraged them to want to improve, as captured in one interview:

> [Renee] came to my room and observed and gave me positive feedback. She always says something positive. I think that is what we need here. . . . We know there are things we can do better, but there are also things that we are doing well. And that's never acknowledged by anyone. When Renee comes in she says positive things. It's never said by administrators.

Our affirming interactions with teachers—recognition of hard work in a challenging environment—created a place for "learning without fear," as one teacher put it, or as another said, "a safe place to experiment." This security spurred growth for many of the teachers in the partner schools: "My relationship with Patty was the biggest thing. She gave me encouragement, praise. She'd say, 'You're doing great things in here. Let me show you these other things to take it a step further.' I'm a much better teacher because of it."

From the evaluation, it became clear that our approach to partnering had been very meaningful to teachers, and they confirmed the importance of all three major precepts of the enabling approach to what they viewed as the successes of the project. We need to note, though, that the evaluation was not designed to systematically correlate implementation of the enabling approach to specific changes in schools or classrooms. Through the open-ended interviews and other evaluation activities, we wanted to learn what teachers thought about how we had worked with them, which interventions they found useful, and what they wish we had done differently.

WHAT TO DO NEXT TIME: GIVE TEACHERS EVEN MORE

One of the most consistent findings across schools was teachers' desire for more interaction with project staff. This finding was true across the entire spectrum of teachers, from those who were overwhelmingly supportive of the Schools Project to those who were not particularly enthusiastic. Often the desire for more interaction was linked to the high quality of training provided through the project:

[The Schools Project staff have] a genuineness and, I think, a high level of expertise . . . and I think many of us recognize these as being important. There are lots of external partners that sort of breeze through here, and we look at them and say, "Tell me something that I don't already know." And when there's something out there that we don't know about and it's useful, many of us are clamoring and want more and more and more.

Some differences emerged among teachers in the evaluation as to the type of interaction they wanted more of. Newer teachers not surprisingly wanted more in-service training opportunities; teachers who had not participated in the project's in-depth, extended training courses—for example, for the Responsive Classroom approach—saw colleagues who had participated reaping benefits and wanted the opportunity, too; and teachers who had visited other classrooms or schools with project staff for observation of successful practices felt that more visits would help them develop further.

Beyond these subgroup differences, teachers generally shared a desire for more one-on-one contact with project staff in their own classrooms during the regular school day, to receive individualized assistance to implement what they were learning through the project. "I wish that I would have more time to spend with Renee," said a teacher. "Just to have her here observing, not just one day. I would like her to come in when the kids are not at their best, come in for, like, one week."

In the evaluation, one week was generally the time frame for one-on-one consultations that teachers came up with when asked how they'd balance their need for individual support with our obligation to assist other teachers in the school as well. In the Schools Project, we devoted considerable time to in-class demonstrations and one-on-one consultations, but one continuous week in each classroom would not have been possible. It is interesting to consider, however, how a partnership could be funded and structured to provide more individualized coaching for teachers.

ADMINISTRATION'S ROLE IN WHOLE-SCHOOL CHANGE

All the administrators interviewed for the evaluation spoke positively about the Schools Project, but ultimately it was difficult for Karen and Ruanda to discern whether they were happy about the actual work of the project or simply pleased to have been the recipient of extra resources. Except for Nolan's principal, whose administrative style included daily contact with students and teachers, and Doyle's principal, who was an Erikson graduate, administrators in the evaluation spoke about the project only in general terms. Though we had actively pursued relationships with principals, the evaluation revealed that most of them viewed the Schools Project as applying only to teachers: They did not speak about their own role in the project.

Ruanda and Karen found clear evidence, however, that administrators strongly influenced the course of partnerships, even if they didn't realize it—a finding that confirmed our own experience over the years. As Ruanda and Karen explored the degree to which the Schools Project had resulted in whole-school change, teachers invariably cited administrative factors that either fostered or constrained the depth and breadth of change in a school.

At Nathan, teachers talked about the administration's bureaucratic decisionmaking process, which contributed to a "negative climate" at the school. Reacting to the school atmosphere, teachers kept to themselves: "Around here," said one Nathan teacher, "the more self-directed you are, the better off you are." With teachers operating in isolation from one another and from administrators, it is not surprising that the Schools Project did not result in schoolwide change at Nathan, but touched only individual classrooms where teachers were receptive.

At the other end of the spectrum was Nolan, which underwent the greatest transformation as a school during the project. The principal at the time the school joined the project was supportive of the endeavor, but the most dramatic changes began to take place in the school upon the arrival of a new principal several years later. In the evaluation, Nolan teachers commented on the difference made by this new administrator, an early childhood champion who participated actively in the partnership.

The other schools in the evaluation fell somewhere between Nathan and Nolan, exhibiting varying degrees of schoolwide change, influenced at least in part by administrative attitudes and actions, some direct and others indirect in relation to the Schools Project. One issue that came up repeatedly in the evaluation was administrators who required teachers to participate in the initiative, a practice we recommended against. When principals mandated teacher participation in the Schools Project, the evaluators generally found that it undermined the partnership. At Trujillo, for example, teachers were mandated to attend weekly early-morning workshops on the Responsive Classroom approach even if they had previously completed the extensive off-site training course. These weekly meetings were not helpful to most teachers—they weren't enough for teachers who hadn't had the off-site training, and they were repetitive for those who had—so teachers felt either frustrated or that their time was being wasted, which weakened their commitment to the initiative.

There was an exception among the schools where participation was mandated. At Nolan, the principal did require all teachers to implement the Responsive Classroom approach, but the mandate was followed by actions that clearly supported implementation and demonstrated commitment. First, the administration cultivated consensus about the value of the Responsive Classroom by communicating to everyone, even parents, the philosophy and purposes of the intervention. Second, the principal did things such as pay teachers stipends for time spent on the intervention above and beyond normal work hours, and she reconfigured the daily schedule to accommodate implementation of components of the Responsive Classroom curriculum. Third, but by no means least important, in her own interactions with staff and students, the principal modeled caring, respect, and other qualities that are central to the Responsive Classroom.

In other schools, however, the evaluation revealed that principals who mandated teacher participation thought they were promoting whole-school change, but in the end it usually backfired, engendering resentment and resistance among some teachers. Pressure to participate often caused teachers to react negatively to us. One teacher said, "[Teachers] would give [project staff] cold shoulders or something like that or go to the principal and say, 'I don't want that person in the class.'" In these schools, the principal's directive was not backed up sufficiently by actions to build understanding and consensus and to integrate the work of the project into the everyday life of the school, as it had been at Nolan.

THE CONFLUENCE OF IDEOLOGICAL
AND RACIAL DIFFERENCES

One of the most challenging schools for Ruanda and Karen to evaluate was Xavier South. Though the school had been part of the project for all 11 years, change seemed to be limited to some individual teachers' classrooms and did not extend throughout the entire school. In the interviews, Ruanda and Karen tried to explore possible reasons for these limited effects. Many teachers were quick to tell them that the DAP-based approaches we had promoted were inappropriate for the low-income African-American children they taught and that we "assumed too much for [their] children's abilities." As one teacher explained in an interview:

> Well, these children, what kind of experiences have they had? They don't have language experiences in the homes. The parents are on drugs, or there are no parents and the grandparents are raising them, and they're tired. So these children need basics, and that is what we have found out. They need structure.

As we described in chapter 3, the resistance of some teachers to DAP did cause us to reconsider our assumptions about it, particularly in regard to at-risk children, but even as our understanding of DAP evolved, many teachers at Xavier South continued to believe it was a mismatch for their students. Their unwavering ideological stand was particularly striking when compared to the response of Doyle School teachers, whose students were also low-income African-American children living in a drug-ravaged neighborhood. At Doyle, only a few miles from Xavier South, teachers also felt that the children were not "read to and cuddled and worked with at home," yet they readily adopted DAP-based approaches and valued them. One teacher there said, "If I miss a couple of days [of using the Responsive Classroom curriculum], I can tell, I can tell. And so I say, 'Okay, we've got to get back to this.'" Doyle teachers reported to the evaluators that the Responsive Classroom approach had helped them keep children focused and well behaved and had led to a caring and respectful learning environment.

The faculty profiles at Doyle and Xavier South weren't so different—both had a mix of Black and White teachers with a range of experience, both had a Black curriculum coordinator and a Black principal—yet the teachers' responses to DAP in the two schools were virtually opposite. In the evaluation, Karen noted that there were subtle neighborhood differences that might have accounted for the differing ideas at Xavier South and Doyle about what would benefit low-income African-American children. While the two neighborhoods suffer from the same types of inner-city problems, Xavier South's children mostly live in one of Chicago's infamous housing projects, while Doyle's live in smaller multifamily buildings or single-family homes. In studying schools across the city while at the University of Chicago, Karen had found that teachers tend to feel differently about children when they are from public housing projects, believing them to be even more at risk, which could have accounted for Xavier South's belief that students there need a structured, teacher-centered approach.

Moreover, while the principals at Xavier South and Doyle were both committed to improving early childhood education, the evaluators noted that Doyle's principal seemed to have a more natural affinity for, and a better understanding of, DAP, which may have made a difference in how teachers there responded to it. In her evaluation interview, the principal described her arrival at Doyle a decade earlier:

> When I came in, my vision was just to get the school cleaned up. The school was a mess. There was graffiti, and just a lot of problems here at the school. The community only sees what they see, and if they see

a mess, then they think it's a mess. We wanted to impact favorably on the community.

During the interview, she spoke about wanting Doyle to see the community as a resource, not an obstacle. This idea and others she expressed fit well with the philosophy of DAP. However, it is important to remember that Xavier South's principal at the beginning of the partnership, who was not the principal at the time of the evaluation, had been trained as an early childhood educator and was very open to DAP, yet the school's teachers even then were resistant to the pedagogical approach.

Perceptions of race may also have played a role in producing limited change at Xavier South. In the interviews, some teachers said that we were out of touch with the school's needs, and our lack of understanding was attributed to race. Patty, the main project staff person at Xavier South, is White. Some teachers implied that because of her race, she could not fully understand the school's issues, and the presence of African Americans on the project team was not acknowledged as a balancing factor. Also during the evaluation interviews, White teachers at Xavier South spoke off the record about race to Karen, who is White, and Black teachers spoke likewise to Ruanda, who is Black. There seemed to be racial undercurrents at the school that may have existed before the Schools Project even began.

Like Xavier South, Doyle emphasizes Afrocentric learning, and there is a strong awareness of race in the school, yet race was not an issue between school and project staff. At Doyle, there was never a concern that racial differences would weaken the partnership, and teachers there did not differentiate between Black and White project staff. In fact, administrators and teachers were quick to speak of project staff to the evaluators as "intertwined in this school and in our philosophy."

On the surface, Xavier South and Doyle didn't look so different from one another in terms of their students, teachers, or administrators, yet their experiences in the Schools Project were very different. So why did ideology and race become issues at Xavier South but not at Doyle? The evaluators never could precisely account for the contrasting experiences. The primary lesson from a comparison of these two case histories seems to be that it is somewhat unpredictable when factors such as ideology and race will affect the course of a partnership. When embarking on a partnership, everyone needs to be sensitive to these factors, but should not assume that they will play a damaging role, because while they did at Xavier South, they did not at Doyle.

INDIVIDUAL TEACHER CHANGE: IT HAPPENED, IT LASTED, AND IT'S IMPORTANT

As part of the evaluation, Ruanda and Karen asked teachers how the Schools Project had most supported them in their professional development, offering them four areas for consideration:

- Conceptual understanding of pedagogical issues
- Skill development
- Implementation of classroom-level changes
- Desire to grow as a teacher

While there was clear evidence from other evaluation activities that many teachers had increased their knowledge and skills and changed their classrooms, teachers themselves felt that the Schools Project's impact on their professional development was greater in regard to their motivation to improve. Two teachers' comments reflect this strongly held opinion among their colleagues:

> I think Erikson's impact came through the desire to change. It gave me the ability to change and really see the need to change, and gave me concrete stuff that I could do to change.

> I think developing our desire to change, presenting new ideas and getting turned on by them, people want to change.

Teachers' desire to improve lasted over time, even beyond the life of the partnership, as evidenced by teacher interviews in schools that had left the project years earlier. For these teachers, the Schools Project was a springboard for continuing professional development: "We started nine years ago with Erikson," said one teacher, "and we're still doing it. . . . Erikson opened the door for other professional development to work with us."

The majority of teachers surveyed for the evaluation indicated that the Schools Project had helped them change in various ways as teachers, though the survey data don't capture the extent to which some teachers believed they had changed. As one teacher said, "I've totally changed what I do . . . but it's been very, very gradual, and quite honestly, when [the Schools Project] first came in, it was like, no, you can stay out, Erikson. But Marie said that she'd help pull students in, and then gradually I said, 'Come on in.'"

Many of the project teachers commented that as they learned, practiced, and succeeded with new approaches during the partnership, their increased sense of professional efficacy translated into increased satisfaction with their work:

> I think with their help they exposed me to a lot of different things, and I learned that gradually I could teach other ways than with a basal reader, and I came to realize that I have a pretty good handle on what these kids need to learn, and I feel a lot more positive about my teaching, my interactions with the kids.

From the evaluation, it became clear that even where whole-school change didn't occur, the Schools Project was very successful at supporting teacher-level change. Even at Xavier South, where teachers reacted so negatively to DAP, a surprising number of teachers indicated in the evaluation survey that the project had increased their pedagogical knowledge, motivation to improve, access to materials, and repertoire of instructional strategies; many teachers there also indicated on the survey that they used these strategies regularly in the classroom.

The high degree of teacher-level change during the project is likely a direct reflection of our belief that teachers are critical partners in any school reform effort, because they are directly responsible for children's education. While we always worked with administrators on the process of school improvement, it is fair to say that most of our time and energy during the Schools Project was at the classroom level, with individual teachers. Thus, even in schools where the administration followed through less on its commitment to the project, we were able to help individual teachers realize their goals for supporting children's learning and development.

CHAPTER 9

Responsive Partnering in Context

The Factors That Shape University–School Partnerships

(with Ruanda Garth McCullough)

ERIKSON INSTITUTE'S SCHOOLS PROJECT was a unique, complex, and revealing journey. The project spanned 11 years, incorporating partnerships with nine public elementary schools in Chicago. All the schools served primarily low-income students, but each one was distinctive, because of the racial and ethnic makeup of the student body, the school's pedagogical orientation, or other factors. The diversity of the schools gives us a unique perspective on partnering that a single university–school collaboration could not offer, and the length of many of the partnerships is unusual as well.

Adding to the complexity of the project, it evolved during a period of successive and rapid local school reforms. Foremost among them were the move to local school control in the late 1980s and the swing back to more centralized authority in the mid-1990s, particularly through a test-based academic accountability system. During the project, we concentrated on the effects of these reforms in the partner schools in addition to the partnership-originating goals, which made the work more challenging, yet added relevance and authenticity to our efforts.

The course of the partnerships also reflected changes in the burgeoning field of early childhood education, many of which Erikson Institute was involved in. The Schools Project began alongside, and was deeply influenced by, the emergence of developmentally appropriate practice as a

123

framework for creating quality educational experiences for young children. Consequently, we found ourselves addressing a host of issues that reso-nate strongly today with educators around the country, issues such as whole-language instruction, direct instruction, performance-based assess-ment, standardized testing for accountability purposes, academic stan-dards, and the needs of at-risk children.

A developing child is our favorite metaphor for the Schools Project. Like a young child, it struggled and flourished in the context of the larger world of local and national reform movements, and was nurtured and challenged by our day-to-day relationships with teachers and prin-cipals. Each aspect of the initiative grew in ways we did not anticipate, but over the 11-year course of the project we came to view our work as coherent, and the lessons that emerged shed light not only on the teach-ing and learning process in low-income urban schools, but also on the process by which a university and a school join together to effect school change.

From the Schools Project experience and third-party evaluation, we have derived four types of contextual realities that shape all university–school partnerships:

1. School system supports and pressures
2. The school environment and culture
3. Teacher individuality and diversity
4. The resources and limits of the university

These contextual realities reflect the thick soup of political, institutional, and personal circumstances in which a partnership either sinks or swims. Any of them can at one moment increase the potential for positive school change and at another act as a constraint or obstacle. Moreover, it is rare for all these contextual realities to mesh harmoniously, and for us an im-portant feature of the enabling approach—Erikson's approach to partnering for the project—is that it acknowledges disjunctions and seeks to find points of connection and compromise, to support transformation through collabo-ration rather than compliance (see Figure 9.1).

In this final chapter, we describe each contextual reality as experienced in the Schools Project and make recommendations for navigating them—recommendations that we believe will contribute to the strength and ef-fectiveness of university–school partnerships. The chapter concludes with a reflection on caring, trusting, and respectful relationships, which we consider the key to building a responsive partnership between a school and a university.

FIGURE 9.1. Contextual Realities That Shape University–School Partnerships

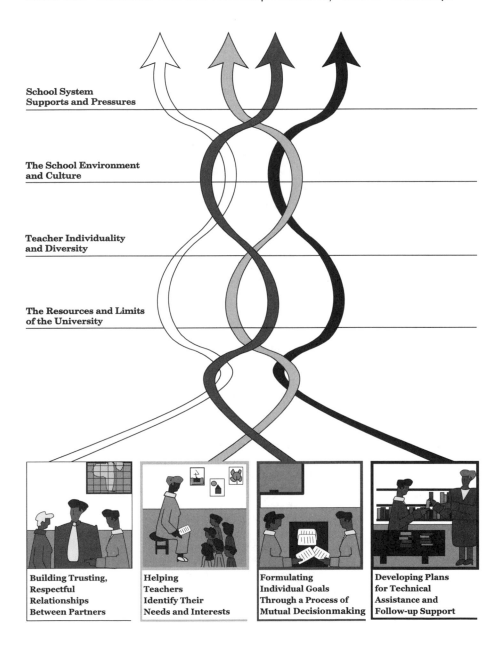

School System
Supports and Pressures

The School Environment
and Culture

Teacher Individuality
and Diversity

The Resources and Limits
of the University

Building Trusting,
Respectful
Relationships
Between Partners

Helping
Teachers
Identify Their
Needs and Interests

Formulating
Individual Goals
Through a Process of
Mutual Decisionmaking

Developing Plans
for Technical
Assistance and
Follow-up Support

SCHOOL SYSTEM SUPPORTS AND PRESSURES

During the project, everyone strongly sensed the presence of the system in the schools, as the board of education worked to implement a host of state and local reform initiatives, many of which indelibly marked the partnerships. There were many points of congruence between these reform initiatives and the goals of the project. In the early 1990s, for example, the state mandated the assessment of learning outcomes through both a standardized achievement test and a performance-based assessment. This policy change neatly coincided with our work in the partner schools to develop alternative assessments. Then, in the mid-1990s, the city board of education developed its own set of learning standards, which set high expectations for student achievement and clarified goals for teaching and learning, strengthening the foundation for the project's work around curriculum and instruction. On another front, CPS efforts to renovate or expand school buildings during the project reduced overcrowding and improved conditions in some of the partner schools, creating an environment more conducive to child-centered learning. And finally, the district's push for school technology development in the 1990s dovetailed with our own technology efforts.

But there were times when the school system and the project were not moving in the same direction, most notably when the city began to use standardized test scores as the measure for school accountability. In the mid-1990s, CPS began judging schools by the percentage of students scoring at or above the national norm on the reading section of the ITBS; schools where fewer than 15% scored at or above the norm were put on academic probation. From our perspective, such high-stakes testing does not represent educational best practice, because consequential decisions about schools, teachers, or students should never be based on a single piece of data. Moreover, there are many questions about whether norm-referenced paper-and-pencil tests like the ITBS fully and accurately measure children's skills and knowledge and whether they are particularly insensitive to differences in gender, culture, and socioeconomic status (Elmore, 2002; Horton & Bowman, 2001; Stiggins, 2002).

But the pressure among teachers and principals for students to perform well on standardized tests was so great, it was inevitable that many of them ended up focusing their energies on improving or maintaining scores, and the pressure was intensified by the knowledge that their jobs could be at stake. In the project schools, this pressure caused many teachers to revert from the developmentally appropriate practices they had begun using back to rote, disembedded learning of facts and skills. This type of learning was even pushed down to the youngest children in many of the schools. Our efforts around NAEYC accreditation for the early child-hood classrooms and the productive use of standardized test scores as an assessment tool at all grade levels were two ways we sought to balance project goals and system requirements. NAEYC accreditation served as a framework for helping teachers and principals understand the benefits of developmentally appropriate practice in comparison to the limits of teaching to the test, and by using test score analyses as an assessment tool in the schools, we were able to open the door for discussion and intervention around a host of curricular and instructional issues, because teachers began to see the connection between test scores and day-to-day classroom practices. Both efforts created inroads for developmentally appropriate practice while fully acknowledging system accountability policies.

Over the 11 years of the Schools Project, there were more than a dozen major educational initiatives, policy changes, and mandates that came down from either the state or city board of education, keeping us in a perpetual dance with the partner schools as we sought to understand their effects on the project and, when necessary, integrate them into the work of the project. Nationwide, an era of intense school reform is under way, and university–school partnerships in the future are likely to find themselves in a situation similar to ours. This first set of recommendations provides general guidance for considering a partnership within the context of the larger school system:

- *Mesh partnership goals with the school system's agenda.* Study the system's agenda carefully when determining goals for a partnership. Where possible, make an effort to link the partnership goals with the system agenda, so that they can reinforce each other. These linkages should be clearly and continuously communicated to school staff, who are likely to be more motivated to invest time and energy in the partnership if they know that working toward its goals will help them meet system goals as well.
- *Move beyond negative assumptions about the school system.* Large, urban school systems like the Chicago Public Schools face myriad challenges, from deciding how to use limited funds, to serving a large number of at-risk children, to meeting government and taxpayer expectations, and particular policies often anger or frustrate one constituency or another. When confronted with policies that do not seem to support the goals of a partnership, it is important to move beyond debating their reasonableness to understanding the complexity of the system and looking for potential allies within it.
- *Be flexible yet tenacious.* Find ways to respond to the requirements of the system, and the anxieties they inspire in teachers and princi-

pals, while keeping sight of what is developmentally best for children. Whenever possible, provide thoughtful counsel to teachers and administrators about how they might blend system requirements and project goals.

THE SCHOOL ENVIRONMENT AND CULTURE

The environment and culture of a school grow out of the particularities of its people and place, mixing in ways that make every school unique. In the Schools Project, aspects of the school environment and culture that most affected the course of the partnerships were the pedagogical philosophy and administrative style of the principal; the school's physical plant; and the characteristics of the community served by the school.

The Principal

A principal's pedagogical philosophy directly influences the school's curriculum and instruction. In schools where the principal strongly supported the principles of DAP and active learning, and where teachers were encouraged to work together in a pleasurable and stimulating environment, not surprisingly, the project was more likely to flourish. Some principals were open to the Schools Project approach but knew little about early childhood education. In these cases, we spent considerable time helping them learn about the field.

Where the principal had a very different approach to education, the partnership floundered or, at best, had lesser effects. In one school, for example, after the partnership was well under way, the principal decided without teacher input to require a direct-instruction approach for reading, all the way down to the kindergarten classrooms. Not only are direct instruction and DAP not entirely compatible, but none of us were well enough versed in direct instruction to offer meaningful technical assistance. In this case, the partnership continued, but at a minimal level.

The administrative style of the principal could also help or hinder the partnership. Principals with an authoritarian style could easily undermine the project, particularly since they were more likely to mandate teachers' participation without cultivating a shared understanding of the purpose of the partnership. Moreover, teachers tended to feel alienated from authoritarian principals, and that alienation usually spilled over to the Schools Project, viewed in these cases simply as an extension of the administration. Also, when there was a lack of communication and understanding between principal and teachers, there was usually the same lack between principal and project staff. An authoritarian principal was just as unlikely to work collaboratively with us as with the teachers.

But too passive a principal was difficult as well. It was not enough just to welcome us into the school and then leave us to do our job. For teachers' buy-in to occur, they needed to see the principal working hand-in-hand with us. When partner schools began to implement the Responsive Classroom approach, for example, the principals all applauded the effort, but many did not follow up with the types of administrative support that would help the intervention take root, such as paying stipends to teachers for meetings outside their normal workday or reorganizing the daily schedule to better accommodate the components of the Responsive Classroom.

Sometimes principals were too keen on the idea of partnerships and engaged in one or more in addition to the Schools Project. Other partners might include museums, social service agencies, or businesses, and though these partnerships' goals at times complemented those of the project, simultaneous partnerships usually resulted in a lack of focus within the school and competition for limited teacher time.

The School Building

A school's physical environment can be a powerful influence on the educational process, and severe overcrowding was a serious problem at some of the partner schools. For the Schools Project, insufficient space in these schools made it difficult to create a child-centered environment where students could actively explore materials or engage in small-group activities, two common elements of developmentally appropriate practice. One school tried to relieve the overcrowding by moving some classrooms to a satellite site. While this solution provided some teachers and students with more space, it made communication among teachers, administrators, and project staff more difficult, and the school began to feel fragmented.

In two other project schools, outdoor play was not possible. One school was located in a neighborhood where gang shootings occurred almost daily, so it was unsafe to play outside. One year, parents in the school made a quilt with 15 names on it, commemorating the children under the age of 18 who had been killed in the neighborhood during the past 5 years. At the other school, located in an old church building, there was no playground, and nowhere to build one. In both these schools, we worked with administrators and teachers to create an indoor play space designated particularly for young children, rearranging either the gym or the cafeteria.

The Community

The racial and ethnic profile of the student body is another significant element of the school environment and culture. Some of the partner schools were primarily African American or Latino, while others had a mix of students—White, Black, Latino, and Asian. In our society, race and ethnicity can sometimes come to represent a barrier to achievement. Along with teachers, we sought to make sure that each child's background represented something positive, building on the rich heritage of the students to make learning culturally relevant, for example, by supporting the development of an Afrocentric curriculum.

Other aspects of the communities served by the partner schools reflected the serious problems common to poor urban neighborhoods: gang violence, child neglect and abuse, housing instability, and poor health, to name just a few. Many of these problems were beyond the ability of teachers or project staff to control, though it was important to acknowledge them and, when possible, ameliorate them. Our attempts to address some of these issues included implementing the Responsive Classroom approach, supporting parent education and involvement initiatives in the schools, and even organizing events like family night at a local museum. These activities demonstrated the belief of the Schools Project that improving young children's educational opportunities requires more than just addressing curricula and instruction. It also requires understanding the community and family context, building on its positive aspects, and, when possible, providing supports to counteract any negative aspects.

Other partnerships may not be affected by the same features of the school environment and culture as those that were so influential in the Schools Project, though this contextual reality, in one way or another, will play a role in every partnership. We have tried to generalize from our experience to formulate several recommendations in this area:

- *Identify the impetus for the partnership.* Why a school is engaging in a partnership can make a huge difference in how the partnership unfolds. Did the school board mandate the partnership? Was it the principal's idea? The teachers'? Where is the motivation for change coming from? The answers to these questions should help a university identify possible sources of cooperation and resistance.
- *Assess the school's readiness for the partnership.* To benefit from a partnership, a school must be in a certain state of readiness. *Readiness* in this sense does not imply a school's higher state of institutional functioning, but the compatibility between the school's and university's pedagogical approaches, and the school's openness to experiment-

ing with new ideas and strategies. The greater the distance between approaches, and the more reluctant a school is to experiment, the less likely it is that positive changes will take place in the school.

- *Understand the school's vision of professional development.* All schools have traditions regarding professional development. In designing interventions and technical assistance, the university needs to take these traditions into account. This includes identifying and working with those individuals in the school who support the process, among either teachers or administrators, and understanding whether and how consensus for change is achieved.
- *Look beyond the school.* For school change to come about, it is usually critical to involve parents and make connections to families. Similarly, understanding the strengths and needs of the larger community can make a difference in the outcomes of a partnership.
- *Pay attention to the unique personality of each partner school before promoting a network.* The Schools Project was unusual for a partnership initiative because it included more than one school. A partnership network can be a wonderful vehicle for helping schools learn from and support one another. Because every school has its own environment and culture, however, the university must expect that each relationship with a school will be different and should respond to the individuality of each school before building on their commonalities.

TEACHER INDIVIDUALITY AND DIVERSITY

In the classroom, it is teachers who make the minute-to-minute decisions each day, and no matter what policies are passed, what reforms are mandated, in the end educational change is in the hands of teachers. For this reason, the success of any partnership depends on the degree to which the university works respectfully and knowledgeably with teachers, and just as no two schools are alike, teachers vary greatly in their training and expertise and in their beliefs and motivation.

In any public school, it is possible to find teachers across the pedagogical spectrum: some are veterans, some are fresh from school; some have been trained traditionally, some progressively; some hold integrationist views about the education of children of color, some have a separatist philosophy; some try to integrate computer technology into the classroom, some push computers out of the classroom and into the hallway. To work effectively with such a diversity of teachers in a single school, we sought to understand their pedagogical beliefs and how they played out in the classroom, discerning the kind of support each would need to engage in reflective practice and professional inquiry.

Coupled with teachers' pedagogical diversity is their psychological diversity. While some teachers welcomed project staff, others resented us and felt threatened by our presence in the school. Just by virtue of being a teacher in the "worst" school system in the nation, many Schools Project teachers felt that their professionalism was automatically called into question by people who did not know the context of their work. Adding to the strain, since the 1995 Chicago school reform legislation, the system has focused more on "sticks" than "carrots" to motivate teachers. The efforts of Chicago's teachers are rarely celebrated, and once teachers begin to feel that they will not be rewarded for their efforts, it is common for them to resist the type of change that is represented by an initiative like the Schools Project (Bryk, Thum, Easton, & Luppescu, 1998; Moore, 1990). More than once we heard, "Who are you to tell me how to do my job?" "There is no reason for me to change." "I don't care what you say, I'll do things my way." "Tomorrow they will change the rules. I'm not going to change today and have to go back tomorrow." Attitudes like these made building trusting, respectful relationships the essential first step in the partnerships.

In response to teacher individuality and diversity, we played multiple roles as partners. We were always listeners: being attentive as they talked about what they were already doing in the classroom, what they wanted to do, what they were worried about, what they thought of each phase of the project. We were sometimes co-workers: teaching beside them in the classroom, modeling strategies in their classrooms, exploring new techniques and ideas together. We were certainly facilitators: constantly looking for evidence of effective practice in classrooms and using our observations to frame reflective discussions and make plans with teachers. Common to all these roles were our personal interactions with individual teachers; where there was initial distrust toward us as partners, it often could be broken down through these one-on-one interactions.

Of the four contextual realities, we have the most recommendations in regard to teacher individuality and diversity, reflecting the foremost role that teachers play in bringing about school change:

- *Work with teachers as true partners and never treat them as a problem.*
  Though the adage admonishes to "never say never," in this we are confident: Never walk into a school assuming that teachers are the problem there. The ultimate success of the partnership depends on how sincerely university staff treat teachers as real partners, listen-

ing to them, taking their concerns and suggestions seriously, and supporting them whenever and wherever possible.

- *Begin with willing teachers and allow the good word to spread.* The positive experiences of volunteers, spread by word of mouth, are usually more successful than a mandate for engaging initially reticent or disinterested teachers. Success tends to breed success.
- *Recognize teachers' differing types of training and levels of experience.* New teachers may have training in more current educational theories and practices, but they have limited classroom experience. Veteran teachers may be less well versed in newer ideas and strategies, but they have years of hands-on expertise. Teachers' differences in experience and training, and in other areas as well, need to be acknowledged and addressed in the partnership process, particularly when creating professional development opportunities.
- *Incorporate teachers' successful practices into new interventions.* Incorporating what already works in the classroom not only builds bridges between the known and the new for teachers, but it also makes them feel valued and respected.
- *Provide specific, concrete technical assistance.* While many teachers appreciate learning about new ideas and theories, they really appreciate it when the ideas and theories are connected to actual classroom techniques and strategies. It is important to model these practices and to give teachers a chance to try them in their own classrooms, offering feedback and providing opportunities for individual consultation.
- *Acknowledge the day-to-day realities of teachers' work.* A university partner may not be able to eliminate a testing requirement or reduce the size of a class, but honest and empathic recognition of these realities builds trust, which in turn builds commitment to the partnership.
- *Provide teachers with options.* Offering choices to teachers at different points throughout the partnership gives them the chance to be engaged in ways that are personally meaningful and that reflect their individual strengths and interests, thereby promoting real shifts in thinking and practice.
- *If targeting specific groups of teachers, don't forget the rest of the school.* A partnership may be focused on a particular group of teachers in a school, such as early childhood teachers. In these cases, try to build bridges between the partnership teachers and others in the school, so that at the very least there is a shared understanding of the work of the partnership. The other teachers may even get drawn into the

partnership or become motivated to pursue their own professional development activities.

THE RESOURCES AND LIMITS OF THE UNIVERSITY

It is important to recognize what the university brings—or does not bring—to the partnership. Different types of external partners have different resources to offer a school. A business, for example, might provide direct financial assistance or materials such as computers for an initiative a school is undertaking. Other partners might be more actively involved in the initiative, providing personnel to tutor children or assist teachers with specific activities. In the case of universities, they usually bring some form of expert technical assistance, coupled with financial support, to a partnership. Whatever the type of external partner, however, the nature of the resources and how they are offered always reflect its institutional structure and identity.

As a graduate school and research center, Erikson had to apply to philanthropic foundations for funding to support the Schools Project. The proposal-writing process for foundations requires the applicant to identify issues or problems, present an intervention to address them, and describe how the intervention will be evaluated. This meant that Erikson had to commit to using grants for specific purposes. We consulted with partner schools when writing proposals—except for the original project proposal, which was written before CPS chose the initial schools—but as the history of the Schools Project makes clear, the partnership goals often changed over time. Though the proposal agenda was sometimes broad enough to incorporate a newly emergent goal, it was not always the case, and we could not simply reallocate foundation grants for a new intervention. Partner schools did not always understand these funding restrictions, and there were a few instances when a school felt resentment at not being able to use grant money however it wished. When possible and appropriate to the partnership, we would pursue a new grant for a particular purpose, but this is usually a relatively slow process, so the money was never available immediately.

There were also limits to the types of technical assistance Erikson could offer the partner schools. Erikson Institute's field of expertise is early childhood development and education, particularly in the areas of learning theory, emergent literacy, and parents' role in young children's learning. Initially in the Schools Project, we worked only with early childhood classrooms, especially on preliteracy development, but many of the partner schools began to ask us to work with older children—and in areas like computer technology—and we knew we were not prepared to provide adequate advice and assistance.

We compensated for the limits of our expertise by expanding the regular project staff and also by hiring consultants to work on specific aspects of the project. For example, we hired a reading specialist to provide support for teachers of older children, and a technology expert to help schools integrate computers into the teaching and learning process. The insights and efforts of the additional staff and consultants dramatically increased the range and quality of technical assistance available through the project. Nonetheless, it was not always easy to bring new people into the project, particularly consultants. Because of the focused nature and relatively short duration of their contribution, it was not always easy for consultants to see how their work fit into the project as a whole, and their relationships with teachers were more tenuous.

Cultural and linguistic differences were another significant factor affecting Erikson's ability to provide appropriate technical assistance. For example, two of the partner schools had a large Latino population and wanted to develop a bilingual curriculum. While some of us spoke Spanish, none of us had strong enough cultural knowledge or the domain expertise to do it, and at our suggestion both schools sought other assistance to meet this need.

In some of the predominantly African-American schools, we had to fight the perception that Erikson was a White institution that could not understand the issues of a non-White classroom or school. This was particularly an issue around developmentally appropriate practice, which some teachers considered inappropriate for disadvantaged children of color. In fact, our project staff did include African Americans, who usually were able to serve as liaisons, helping both sides of the partnership better understand and appreciate a variety of cultural values, beliefs, and practices and lessening any racial dissonance.

Just like any partner school, a university has its own environment and culture and its own staff individuality and diversity. To ensure that we were aware of how these were affecting the course of the partnerships, we engaged in an ongoing process of self-reflection, similar to the process we were asking the schools to undertake. This process took shape in a number of ways: through weekly project staff meetings; continuous internal formative and summative evaluations; periodic meetings with school administrators and teachers; and the third-party evaluation of the project. The self-reflective process resulted not only in an increased ability to be responsive to the partner schools, but also in significant growth and change for Erikson as an institution and for each of us as individuals, in our ideas about partnerships, urban schools, developmentally appropriate practice, professional development, and scores of other issues.

Representing the university side of university–school partnerships, we have a heightened awareness of our role and responsibilities in promoting a productive relationship:

- *Have credibility in the type of school in the partnership.* Project staff should have experience in the type of school with which they are partnering. Otherwise, teachers and administrators may question staff's approach and judgment. Relatedly, it is helpful to have at least some project staff who have cultural backgrounds similar to those of teachers and students, to diminish culturally based misunderstandings or mistrust. Race is perhaps the most sensitive issue today in our country, and it may come into play in university–school partnerships.
- *Be visible and available but know when to step back.* Occasional meetings or workshops do not constitute a partnership. Project staff need to be visible in the school and readily available. On the other hand, staff need to be willing to step back, or even bow out of the picture, when individual teachers or the school indicate a desire to take ownership of an idea.
- *Communicate regularly, openly, and sensitively.* Communication, of course, is a two-way street, but the university partner should set an example of regular, open, and sensitive communication, encouraging everyone involved in the partnership to share their expectations, ideas, and points of view. When there are differences of opinion expressed, the university partner may well have to take the initiative to help people understand and resolve them.
- *Conduct ongoing internal evaluation.* The results of an external evaluation are often long in coming, and sometimes they're not in hand until after the initiative being evaluated is over. So while the findings from an external evaluation are extremely valuable, it is just as important to set up a process for ongoing internal evaluation during the course of a partnership. Particularly because the needs and circumstances of a school can change, ongoing internal evaluation is critical to readjusting goals and keeping the partnership on track or, if necessary, ending it.
- *Engage in reflective practice.* As much as project staff need to be aware of a school's contextual realities, they must also understand those of their own institution and how they influence the partnership in both positive and negative ways. Further, just as staff should evaluate how a school is changing over the course of a partnership, they should consider how they themselves are changing as well.

RELATIONSHIP: THE KEY TO UNIVERSITY–SCHOOL PARTNERSHIPS

University–school partnerships are being promoted more and more frequently as a vehicle for improving public schools in the United States (Barnett, Hall, Berg, & Camerena, 1999; Berliner, 1997; Horsch, 1992; Maeroff, Callan, & Usdan, 2001; Sparks, 2000). Our volume adds to a growing body of literature on the topic, and there is significant agreement about many of the factors that contribute to successful partnerships: among them, joint planning and mutual understanding of goals and outcomes, realistic expectations, strong leadership and commitment, attention to the local context, open and honest communication, and a focus on collaboration (Carriuolo, 1991; Gross, 1988; Mitchell, 2002; Osguthorpe, Harris, Harris, & Black, 1995; Ravid & Handler, 2001; Sadovnik & Semel, 2001; Sirotnik & Goodlad, 1988; Trubowitz & Longo, 1997; Zetlin & MacLeod, 1995).

Our recommendations echo these themes and add some new ones, but what we keep coming back to—what is missing in other writing on university–school partnerships—is the recognition of relationship as the foundation on which all partnership activities rest. Without a strong relationship between university and school, most of the recommendations made by us, or others, cannot be put into action, and the potential of the partnership can never be realized.

What Is Relationship?

Relationship is the process as well as the product of human connections, of regular interaction between individuals in the course of family life, school, work, community involvement, and play. The nature and quality of relationships from infancy on up are critical factors in a person's developmental trajectory. How people feel about themselves and the world, how they learn, how they react to change, how they cope with adversity—all of these qualities and more are influenced by, and often mediated through, relationships. Being connected to other people is fundamental to human nature (Aristotle, 1946; Bowlby, 1958; Dewey, 1963; Erikson, 1950; Evans, 1993; Harlow & Zimmerman, 1959).

Head Start's enabling approach, adapted by Erikson Institute as the partnering approach for the Schools Project and resonant of Erikson's philosophy of teacher education (Stott & Bowman, 1996), recognizes the transformative power of relationships. One of the main tenets of the enabling approach is that the quality of the relationship between a school and the external partner is directly related to the quality of school growth and change that occurs. For this reason, establishing and maintaining personal-professional relationships with teachers in the partner schools was central to our efforts over the entire course of the 11-year project.

As sentimental as it may sound, we sought to make caring the heart of these relationships. We did so for several unsentimental reasons. First, it helped us to suspend judgment about teachers' reactions to the partnership and to work harder to better understand them—their fears and beliefs, desires and experiences. Second, caring relationships seemed the surest route to the type and intensity of collaboration we envisioned for the partnerships. And finally, caring about teachers and the work they do every day simply seemed to us to be the right thing to do.

Suspending Judgment

In a university–school partnership, welcome, acceptance, and cooperation are all possible responses from teachers, but so are resistance and rejection. A very human reaction to resistance or rejection is to make judgments—to pigeonhole, to classify, to patronize—but this attitude forecloses the possibility of progress toward school improvement (Schaps & Lewis, 1999; Tyack & Cuban, 1995). A caring attitude opens the door to the suspension of judgment, to being receptive to other people's perspectives and trying to see things through their eyes. This is easier said than done, but we strove to do it, knowing that an understanding of the sources of teachers' reactions would force us to reconsider our own assumptions about what the schools needed, leading to better-matched intervention plans and technical assistance.

Being able to suspend judgment requires a strong sense of respect—an acknowledgment of the other person's worth and dignity. In the context of the project, this translated into believing in the competency of teachers to carry out their professional responsibilities; being willing to work together courteously and politely; remembering that everyone in the partnership was motivated by a desire to do what was in the best interest of children; and, finally, accepting as legitimate teachers' thoughts and feelings and integrating them with standards of professional practice (Stott & Bowman, 1996).

Promoting Collaboration

Relationships built on care create an environment for collaborative work, because "when we care, we want to do our best for the objects of our care" (Nodding, 1995, p. 25). Moreover, relationships built on care are imbued with an enduring character, which allows the collaboration to be dynamic and "becoming"—a living, growing thing (Buber, 1957). This is exactly how we envisioned the partnerships: We wanted to create an authentic and meaningful discourse with teachers and to make them an integral part of the project, resulting in a responsiveness between partners that would push the initiative to keep evolving and improving.

Collaboration allows for the co-construction of knowledge and stimulates examination of current practice through ongoing inquiry and reflection (Stott & Bowman, 1996). Through collaboration, not only would teachers in the partner schools be stimulated to grow and change, we believed, but we would as well. In this book, we have traced some of the changes that we ourselves underwent, particularly in regard to our understanding of developmentally appropriate practice. But perhaps the greatest change in us brought about by the collaborative experience was in our feelings about the degree of collaboration we desired in a university–school partnership. We'd undertaken the Schools Project intending to promote meaningful collaboration with schools, as envisaged through the enabling approach. In future partnerships, we would want to go even beyond the enabling approach, building on strong personal relationships with teachers and administrators to create a true community of school reformers who together explore new ideas, question one another, and examine assumptions about the teaching and learning process—a vision of "school as an experiment in democracy" (Levine, Lowe, Peterson, & Tenorio, 1995). There were moments during the Schools Project when we achieved this higher level of collaboration, but as we were reminded several times during the project, true collaboration cannot be forced or mandated. A desire and willingness to collaborate is gradually nurtured through personal interactions that exhibit caring, trust, and respect for ideas and approaches different from one's own. When the distance between partners' ideas and approaches is vast, a caring relationship can pave the way for discussion and reflection that lessen the distance, allowing for the development and pursuit of common goals. Sometimes, though, even a caring relationship cannot overcome differences enough to lead to a truly collaborative partnership.

The Right Thing to Do

Teaching, particularly in a poor urban neighborhood, is an intense experience: sometimes joyful, often overwhelming, always challenging. It can also be lonely. To persevere under these circumstances and continue to grow professionally, teachers need "someone with whom to focus, investigate, and brainstorm; someone with whom to share experiences and reactions; someone to be a model and to mirror the emerging professional self" (Shahmoon-Shanok, 1991, p. 16). We wanted to fill this role for the Schools Project teachers, and as we did, teachers felt less isolated and anxious, more comfortable and willing to take risks.

Through our relationships with teachers, we tried to create a safe place for them to explore ideas and feelings, reflect on experiences, and simply enjoy the companionship of another adult. The relationships developed as much through small, casual interactions as through formal meetings and activities: stopping in the hallway or teachers' lounge for a few minutes of conversation; congratulating a teacher on a successfully completed project; helping to clean up a classroom at the end of the day; a simple smile of acknowledgment or a nod of agreement. These little things went a long way toward lessening the distance between partners and conveying a desire to connect. There was no one way to build a relationship, however; much depended on the individuals involved.

Relationship in and of itself is not an easily measurable outcome, and we have no evidence directly correlating the nature and quality of our relationships with teachers to more readily quantifiable outcomes like the implementation of new teaching strategies in the classroom or increases in students' test scores. Our willingness to devote so much time and energy to the relationship-building process during the partnerships, even when our attempts were rebuffed, stemmed from a deep belief that caring relationships are an essential part of the educational process, a means as well as an end. They are a means because people learn and grow when they feel appreciated, understood, and supported, whether an adult or a child, a teacher or a student. There is an exquisitely delicate connection between the positive regard of other people that confers self-esteem and the ability to achieve ever-higher goals. And caring relationships are an end because they model a parallel process in which teachers must engage: with children, with parents, with other teachers, with administrators. For teachers, effectiveness depends as much on their willingness and ability to connect with children, families, and colleagues as it does on their expertise in curriculum and instruction.

Profiles of the Schools Project Team Members

TABLE A. Profiles of the Schools Project Team Members

Name	Role	Phases Worked on Project	Areas of Expertise	Primary Schools
Barbara Bowman	Co-director	1 and 2	• Early literacy, math, and science • School leadership and policy • Multicultural curricula • Technology	All schools during phases 1 and 2
Patty Horsch	Co-director	1, 2, and 3	• Early literacy, math, and science • Social-emotional development • Alternative assessment • School leadership • Professional development	All schools but primarily Ivy, Nolan, and Xavier South
Jie-Qi Chen	Co-director	2 and 3	• Assessment • Program evaluation • Technology	All schools during phases 2 and 3
Deirdre Graziano	Project staff	1	• Early literacy • Professional development	Elston, Ivy, and Newley/Stanton
Jill Bradley	Project staff	1	• Early literacy • Parental involvement • Professional development	Elston, Ivy, and Newley/Stanton
Daria Zvetina	Project staff	2	• Social-emotional development • Professional development	Elston and Wheaton
Renee Salahuddin	Project staff	2 and 3	• Literacy • Parental involvement • Professional development • Afrocentric curricula	Doyle, Newley/Stanton, and Trujillo
Marie Donovan	Project staff	2 and 3	• Literacy • Curriculum and instruction • Assessment • Professional development	Trujillo, Wheaton, and Xavier South
Elizabeth Beyer	Project staff	2 and 3	• Technology • Professional development	All schools during phases 2 and 3
Julie Walstra	Project staff	3	• Technology • Professional development	All schools during phase 3
Warren Dym	Project staff	3	• Technology • Professional development	All schools during phase 3
Gail Burnford	Consultant	3	• Literacy • Curriculum and instruction	Doyle
Christine Davis	Consultant	3	• Literacy • Curriculum and instruction	Wheaton
Joan Berger	Consultant	3	• NAEYC accreditation	All schools during phase 3

Profiles of the Schools Project Partner Schools

TABLE B.1. Descriptive Data on the Partner Schools

	Newley/ Stanton	Nathan	Trujillo	Elston	Ivy	Nolan	Doyle	Wheaton	Xavier South
Partnership duration	2 years (89–91)	3 years (95–98)	3 years (95–98)	4 years (87–91)	4 years (87–91)	7 years (91–98)	9 years (89–98)	9 years (87–96)	11 years (87–98)
Grades in school	pre-K–3	pre-K–7	pre-K–6	pre-K–6	pre-K–8	pre-K–6	pre-K–8	pre-K–8	pre-K–4
Number of students									
At Schools Project entry	853	871	340	661	983	539	853	1,293	742
At Schools Project exit	674	1,217	350	660	1,027	585	688	1,289	499
Race/ethnicity of students									
African American									
At Schools Project entry	8%	83%	3%	100%	8%	4%	100%	28%	100%
At Schools Project exit	9%	91%	7%	100%	6%	6%	100%	34%	100%
Latino									
At Schools Project entry	84%	13%	96%	0%	32%	42%	0%	71%	0%
At Schools Project exit	86%	7%	93%	0%	28%	66%	0%	65%	0%
Asian									
At Schools Project entry	1%	1%	0%	0%	25%	13%	0%	0%	0%
At Schools Project exit	1%	0%	0%	0%	39%	4%	0%	0%	0%
White									
At Schools Project entry	7%	3%	1%	0%	35%	39%	0%	1%	0%
At Schools Project exit	4%	2%	0%	0%	27%	24%	0%	1%	0%
Native American									
At Schools Project entry	0%	0%	0%	0%	0%	2%	0%	0%	0%
At Schools Project exit	0%	0%	0%	0%	0%	0%	0%	0%	0%
Low-income students									
At Schools Project entry	100%	92%	97%	92%	80%	60%	87%	100%	100%
At Schools Project exit	100%	94%	96%	98%	82%	81%	99%	98%	95%

144

Students with limited English proficiency								
At Schools Project entry	37%	10%	89%	0%	13%	14%	0%	20%	0%
At Schools Project exit	32%	3%	68%	0%	21%	26%	0%	17%	0%
Average annual student mobility rate during partnership	n/a	36%	20%	56%	25%	32%	51%	42%	45%
Average annual teacher turnover rate during partnership	n/a	16%	39%	n/a	8%	7%	13%	13%	12%
Principal turnover during partnership	no	no	yes (1995)	no	no	yes (1996)	yes (1998)	yes (1994)	yes (1991)

Source: Chicago Public Schools.

145

TABLE B.2. Schools Project Intervention Areas and Activities, by Partner School

	Newley/Stanton	Nathan	Trujillo	Elston	Ivy	Nolan	Doyle	Wheaton	Xavier South
Partnership duration (years)	2	3	3	4	4	7	9	9	11
Curricula, instruction, and professional community									
Taught course on literacy-based reading		*	*			*	*	*	*
Conducted reading workshops and provided follow-up support						*		*	*
Conducted writing workshops and provided follow-up support	*		*	*	*	*		*	*
Organized Math Their Way workshop and provided follow-up support		*	*			*	*	*	*
Assisted teachers with curriculum development in reading, math, social studies, and integrated units			*	*	*	*	*	*	*
Helped organize and facilitate school math committee						*			
Helped develop and implement Afrocentric curriculum					*		*		*
Helped develop and implement dual-language curriculum			*						
Facilitated visits to other classrooms and other schools	*	*	*	*	*	*	*	*	*
Assisted teachers with classroom arrangement and organization	*	*	*	*	*	*	*	*	*
Organized workshops to introduce children's literature	*			*	*	*	*	*	*
Helped purchase books to build classroom libraries	*	*	*	*	*	*	*	*	*
Helped facilitate grade-level meetings	*	*	*	*	*	*	*	*	*
Worked with teachers on presentations for local and national conferences			*			*	*	*	*
Assessment									
Organized and conducted assessment workshops			*			*	*	*	*
Helped teachers develop assessment rubrics		*	*			*	*	*	*
Worked with teachers to develop report cards		*	*			*	*	*	*
Assisted teachers in creating student portfolios			*			*	*	*	*
Introduced computer software to facilitate assessment of particular projects			*			*			*
Developed methods for using standardized test scores as an assessment instrument			*			*	*		*

	Newley/Stanton	Nathan	Trujillo	Elston	Ivy	Nolan	Doyle	Wheaton	Xavier South
Partnership duration (years)	2	3	3	4	4	7	9	9	11
NAEYC accreditation									
Introduced concept and process of accreditation to administrators, teachers, and parents	*	*				*	*	*	*
Conducted classroom observations and provided follow-up support to meet NAEYC criteria	*	*				*	*		*
Helped prepare parent handbook	*	*				*	*		*
Coordinated CPR and first aid training	*	*				*	*		*
Helped teachers complete required paperwork for accreditation	*	*				*	*		*
Served as validation intermediaries between school and NAEYC	*	*				*	*		*
The Responsive Classroom approach									
Guided introductory discussion sessions on approach to lay foundation for training						*			
Organized training workshops on approach for teachers, administrators, and parents	*	*				*	*	*	*
Offered on-site training on approach	*	*				*	*	*	*
Provided ongoing classroom support to implement approach	*	*				*	*	*	*
Worked with administrators to restructure school day to promote implementation of approach	*					*	*	*	*
Facilitated administrators' and teachers' participation in leadership institutes on approach	*	*				*	*		*
Trained Responsive Classroom facilitators			*			*			
Computer technology									
Helped purchase computer hardware and software	*	*				*	*	*	*
Built software library for school	*	*				*	*		*
Offered computer training sessions to teachers	*	*				*	*	*	*
Worked with teachers on integration of computer technology into teaching and assessment	*	*				*	*	*	*
Conducted leadership seminar for school computer coordinators	*	*				*	*		*
Assisted computer coordinators in developing and conducting teacher and parent courses at school	*	*				*	*		*
Assisted computer coordinators in drafting school technology plans	*	*				*	*		*
Connected teachers and schools through the Internet	*	*				*	*		*

APPENDIX C

Selected Survey Data from the Schools Project Evaluation

TABLE C.1. Teachers' Opinions on the Relevance of the Schools Project

Area of need	Good	Average	Weak	No experience with Schools Project
Schools Project met school's needs	49.8%	25.5%	6.6%	18.2%
Schools Project met classroom's needs	54.4%	25.8%	11.3%	8.1%
Schools Project met students' needs	49.2%	27.4%	14.9%	9.4%

Source: Survey data from the Schools Project evaluation.

Note: Distributions may not add to 100.0% because of rounding.

TABLE C.2. Teachers' Opinions on the Expertise of Schools Project Staff

Area of expertise	Good	Average	Weak	No experience with Schools Project
Technology integration	49.1%	29.6%	3.4%	17.9%
Classroom management	53.9%	22.6%	11.0%	12.6%
Literacy development	54.1%	19.0%	11.3%	15.6%
Teaching techniques	57.0%	19.8%	4.7%	18.5%
Student support	56.9%	19.9%	6.6%	16.6%
Assessment	53.2%	20.2%	10.9%	15.7%
Whole-school development	56.3%	18.0%	10.4%	15.3%
Urban teaching context	49.6%	21.5%	5.8%	23.4%

Source: Survey data from the Schools Project evaluation.

Note: Distributions may not add to 100.0% because of rounding.

TABLE C.3. Teachers' Opinions on the Impact of the Schools Project on Their Professional Development

Area of professional development	Strongly agree/ agree	Neither agree nor disagree	Disagree/ strongly disagree	No experience with Schools Project
Schools Project increased my knowledge	40.7%	36.0%	7.8%	15.5%
Schools Project increased my desire to grow	55.5%	25.3%	9.8%	9.4%
Schools Project increased my access to materials	40.4%	32.1%	13.7%	13.8%
Schools Project taught me useful techniques	50.3%	30.7%	5.2%	13.9%
I use new approaches regularly in the classroom	74.0%	16.5%	9.6%	0.0%

Source: Survey data from the Schools Project evaluation.

Note: Distributions may not add to 100.0% because of rounding.

TABLE C.4. Teachers' Opinions on the Impact of the Schools Project on Whole-School Development

Indication of impact	Strongly agree/ agree	Neither agree nor disagree	Disagree/ strongly disagree	No experience with Schools Project
Enough teachers participated in Schools Project	51.3%	27.1%	8.1%	13.5%
Teachers participated in Schools Project often enough	46.3%	27.7%	15.5%	10.5%
Teachers participated in Schools Project intensely enough	43.5%	28.7%	16.6%	11.1%
My school is a better place because of Schools Project	44.8%	30.1%	14.0%	11.1%

Source: Survey data from the Schools Project evaluation.

Note: Distributions may not add to 100.0% because of rounding.

References

American Educational Research Association. (2000). Position statement of
    American Educational Research Association concerning high-stakes tes
    in preK–12 education. *Educational Researcher, 11*, 24–25.

Anderson, P., Harvey, C., & Pinger, D. (1999, November). *NAEYC's the leading e*
    Paper presented at the annual conference of the National Association for
    Education of Young Children, New Orleans, LA.

Aristotle. (1946). *The politics* (Sir Ernest Barker, Trans.). Oxford, England: Oxf
    University Press.

Association for Supervision and Curriculum Development. (1988). *A resource gi*
    to public school early childhood programs. Alexandria, VA: Author.

Baker, E. L., Herman, J. L., & Gearhat, M. (1989). *The ACOT report card: Effect:*
    complex performance and attitude. Paper presented at the annual conferenc
    the American Educational Research Association, San Francisco, CA.

Banas, C., & Byers, D. (1987, November 7). Chicago's schools hit as worst. *Chic*
    Tribune, p. 1.

Barnett, B., Hall, G., Berg, J., & Camerena, M. (1999). A typology of partners
    for promoting innovation. *Journal of School Leadership, 9*(6), 484–510.

Barnett, W. S. (1995). Long-term effects of an early childhood program on cog
    tive and school outcomes. *The Future of Children, 4*, 25–50.

Barnett, W. S. (1998). Long-term effects on cognitive development and sch
    success. In W. S. Barnett & S. S. Boocock (Eds.), *Early care and education*
    children in poverty: Promises, programs, and long-term outcomes (pp. 11–4
    Albany: State University of New York Press.

Becker, H. J. (2000). Who's wired and who's not: Children's access to and use
    computer technology. *The Future of Children, 10*(2), 44–75.

Berliner, B. (1997). *What it takes to work together: The promise of educational partn*
    ships. San Francisco: WestEd.

Berry, M., & Harris, R. (1998, November). *Making a difference in the quality of p*
    grams through NAEYC accreditation: A successful group-facilitated model in Ro
    ester, New York. Paper presented at the annual conference of the Natioı
    Association for the Education of Young Children, Toronto, Canada.

Beyer, E. (1994). *The five A's: An approach to integrating computers into the classroc*
    Unpublished paper. Chicago: Erikson Institute.

Beyer, E. (1997). *Using technology to construct an effective learning environme*

Paper presented at the annual conference of the American Educational Research Association, Chicago, IL.

Bowlby, J. (1958). The nature of the child's tie to his mother. *International Journal of Psychoanalysis, 39*, 350–373.

Bowman, B. T., Donovan, M. S., & Burns, M. S. (2000). *Eager to learn: Educating our preschoolers.* Washington, DC: National Academy Press.

Bransford, J. D., Brown, A. L., & Cocking, R. R. (Eds.). (1999). *How people learn: Brain, mind, experience, and school.* Washington, DC: National Academy Press.

Bredekamp, S. (Ed.). (1987). *Developmentally appropriate practice in early childhood programs serving children from birth through age 8* (expanded ed.). Washington, DC: National Association for the Education of Young Children.

Bredekamp, S. (1999). When new solutions create new problems: Lessons learned from NAEYC accreditation. *Young Children, 1,* 58–63.

Bredekamp, S., & Copple, C. (Eds.). (1997). *Developmentally appropriate practice in early childhood programs.* Revised edition. Washington, DC: National Association for the Education of Young Children.

Bredekamp, S., & Willer, B. (Eds.). (1996). *NAEYC accreditation: A decade of learning and the years ahead.* Washington, DC: National Association for the Education of Young Children.

Brophy, J., & Good, T. (1986). Teacher behavior and student achievement. In M. Wittrock (Ed.), *Handbook of research on teaching* (pp. 328–375). New York: Macmillan.

Bryk, A. S., Sebring, P. B., Kerbow, D., Rollow, S., & Easton, J. Q. (1999). *Charting Chicago school reform: Democratic localism as a lever for change.* Boulder, CO: Westview Press.

Bryk, A. S., Thum, Y. M., Easton, J. Q., & Luppescu, S. (1998). *Academic productivity of Chicago public elementary schools.* Chicago: Consortium on Chicago School Research.

Buber, M. (1957). *I and thou.* New York: Charles Scribner.

Carriuolo, N. (Ed.). (1991). *Beginning and sustaining school/college partnerships.* Winchester, MA: New England Association of Schools and Colleges.

Carter-Blank, D., & Jor'dan, J. R. (1999). *The McCormick Tribune Foundation's Focus on Quality Initiative: Improving the quality of early childhood education in Chicago's low-income communities.* Paper presented at the annual conference of the National Association for the Education of Young Children, New Orleans, LA.

CEO Forum on Education and Technology. (1997). *School technology readiness report: From pillars to progress.* Washington, DC: Author.

Charney, R. (1991). *Teaching children to care: Management in the responsive classroom.* Greenfield, MA: Northeast Foundation for Children.

Charney, R. (1997). *Habits of goodness: Case studies in the social curriculum.* Greenfield, MA: Northeast Foundation for Children.

Charney, R., Clayton, M., & Wood, R. (1995). *The responsive classroom.* Pittsfield, MA: Northeast Foundation for Children.

Chen, J.-Q., Salahuddin, R., Horsch, P., & Wagner, S. L. (2000). Turning standard-

ized test scores into a tool for improving teaching and learning: An assessment-based approach. *Urban Education, 35*(3), 356–384.

Chicago Board of Education. (1988). *Dropouts: A descriptive review of the class of 1986 and trend analysis of 1982–1986 classes.* Chicago: Author.

Conte, C. (1997). *The learning connection: Schools in the information age.* Washington, DC: Benton Foundation.

Costa, A. L., & Kallick, B. (2000). Getting into the habit of reflection. *Educational Leadership, 4,* 60–62.

Darling-Hammond, L. (1998). Teachers and teaching: Testing policy hypotheses from a national commission report. *Educational Researcher, 27*(1), 5–16.

Darling-Hammond, L., & Sclan, E. (1996). Who teaches and why: Dilemmas of building a profession for 21st-century schools. In J. Sikula, T. Buttery, & E. Guyton (Eds.), *Handbook of research on teacher education* (pp. 67–101). New York: Macmillan.

Delpit, L. (1995). *Other people's children: Cultural conflict in the classroom.* New York: New Press.

Designs for Change. (1982). *Caught in the web: Misplaced children in Chicago's classes for the mentally retarded.* Chicago: Author.

Designs for Change. (1985). *The bottom line: Chicago's failing schools and how to save them.* Chicago: Author.

Dewey, J. (1963). *The school and society.* New York: Macmillan.

Dickinson, D. K. (2002, January/February). Shifting images of developmentally appropriate practice as seen through different lenses. *Educational Researcher,* 26–32.

Downes, T., Arthur, L., & Beecher, B. (2001). Effective learning environments for young children using digital resources: An Australian perspective. *Information Technology in Childhood Education Annual,* 139–154.

Duffrin, E. (1998). Spurring progress: A critical look at Chicago's testing program. *Catalyst: Voices of Chicago Schools Reform, 10*(6), 1–8.

Duffrin, E. (1999). Some do's and some don'ts on keeping teachers. *Catalyst: Voices of Chicago Schools Reform, 11*(1), 15.

Dwyer, D. C., Ringstaff, C., & Sandholtz, J. H. (1991). Changes in teachers' belief and practices in technology-rich classrooms. *Educational Leadership, 23*(1), 15–21.

Early Childhood Education Commission. (1986). *Take a giant step.* New York: Author.

Elmore, R. F. (2002, September–October). Testing trap: The single largest—and possibly most destructive—federal intrusion into America's public schools. *Harvard Magazine, 105,* 35–37, 97.

Erikson, E. H. (1950). *Childhood and society.* New York: Norton.

Evans, R. (1993). The human face of reform. *Educational Leadership, 51* (1), 19–23.

Fein, G. G., & Rivkin, M. (Eds.). (1986). *The young child at play.* Washington, DC: National Association for the Education of Young Children.

Feldman, S. (1998). AFT's role: Bringing vitality to teaching. *Educational Leadership, 55*(5), 19–20.

Filer, R., Heritage, M., & Gallimore, R. (2000). Teachers leading teachers. *Educational Leadership, 4,* 66–69.

Garcia-Coll, C., & Magnuson, K. (2000). Cultural differences as sources of developmental vulnerabilities and resources. In J. P. Shonkoff & S. J. Meisels (Eds.), *Handbook of early childhood intervention* (2nd ed., pp. 94–114). New York: Cambridge University Press.

Garet, M. S., Porter, A. C., Desimone, L., Birman, B. F., & Yoon, K. S. (2001). What makes professional development effective? Results from a national sample of teachers. *American Educational Research Journal, 38*(4), 915–945.

Goffin, S. G. (1988). *Public schools and developmentally appropriate practice: Securing the relationship.* Paper prepared for the National Association of State Boards of Education, Alexandria, VA.

Goldenberg, C. (1994). *Rethinking the means and goals of early literacy education for Spanish-speaking kindergartners.* Paper presented at the annual conference of the American Educational Research Association, New Orleans, LA.

Gross, T. L. (1988). *Partners in education: How colleges can work with schools to improve teaching and learning.* San Francisco: Jossey-Bass.

Haney, W. (2000). The myth of the Texas miracle in education. *Education Policy Analysis Archives, 8*(41), [available on-line at http://epaa.asu.edu/].

Harlow, H. F., & Zimmerman, R. R. (1959). Affectional responses in the infant monkey. *Science, 130,* 421–432.

Hart, B., & Risley, T. R. (1995). *Meaningful difference in the everyday experience of young American children.* Baltimore: Paul H. Brookes.

Hawkins, J., Spielvogel, B., & Panush, E. M. (1996). *National study tour of district technology integration: Summary report.* EDC Center for Children and Technology Report #14. Newton, MA: Education Development Center.

Helburn, S. W. (Ed.). (1995). *Cost, quality, and child outcomes in child care centers: Technical report.* Denver: Center for Research in Economic and Social Policy, University of Colorado.

Heubert, J. P., & Hauser, R. M. (Eds.). (1999). *High stakes: Testing for tracking, promotion, and graduation.* Washington, DC: National Academy Press.

Heywood, J. S., Thomas, M., & White, S. B. (1997). Does classroom mobility hurt stable students? An examination of achievement in urban schools. *Urban Education, 32*(3), 354–372.

Honey, M., Culp, K. M., & Carrigg, F. (2000). Perspectives on technology and education research: Lessons from the past and present. *Journal of Educational Computing Research, 23*(1), 5–14.

Honey, M., & Henriquez, A. (1996). *Union City interactive multimedia education trial: 1993–1995 summary report.* New York: EDC Center for Children and Technology.

Horsch, P. (1992). School change: A partnership approach. *Early Education and Development, 3*(2), 128–138.

Horton, C., & Bowman, B. T. (2001). *Child assessment at the preprimary level: Expert opinion and state trends.* Chicago: Herr Research Center, Erikson Institute.

International Society for Technology in Education. (2002). *National educational technology standards for teachers.* Eugene, OR: Author.

Jacobson, L. (1999, November 10). Early childhood accreditation demand over-whelms NAEYC. *Education Week*, 14–15.

Johnson, S. (1990). *Teachers at work: Achieving success in our schools.* New York: HarperCollins.

Jones, E., & Reynolds, G. (1992). *The play's the thing: Teachers' roles in children's play.* New York: Teachers College Press.

Katz, L. G. (1971). *The enabler model for early childhood programs.* College of Education Curriculum Laboratory, University of Illinois, Urbana, IL (Catalog No. 1360–22).

Katz, L. G. (1987). Early education: What should young children be doing? In S. L. Kagan & E. F. Zigler (Eds.), *Early schooling: The national debate* (pp. 151–167). New Haven: Yale University Press.

Klein, S. P., Hamilton, L., McCaffrey, D., & Stecher, B. M. (2000). *What do test scores in Texas tell us?* Santa Monica, CA: RAND.

Levine, D., Lowe, R., Peterson, R., & Tenorio, R. (Eds.). (1995). *Rethinking schools: An agenda for change.* New York: New Press.

Lewis, C., Schaps, E., & Watson, M. (1996). The caring classroom's academic edge. *Educational Leadership, 51*(1), 16–21.

Linn, R. L. (2000). Assessments and accountability. *Educational Researcher, 29*(2), 4–16.

Maeroff, G. I., Callan, P. M., & Usdan, M. D. (Eds.). (2001). *The learning connection: New partnerships between schools and colleges.* New York: Teachers College Press.

Mallory, B. L., & New, R. S. (Eds.). (1993). *Diversity and developmentally appropriate practices: Challenges for early childhood education.* New York: Teachers College Press.

McGillivray, K. (2000). Educational technologist as curriculum specialist. *Learning and Leading with Technology, 28*(1), 37–41.

McLane, J. B., & McNamee, G. D. (1990). *Early literacy.* Cambridge, MA: Harvard University Press.

Mitchell, S. (Ed.). (2002). *Effective educational partnerships: Experts, advocates, and scouts.* Westport, CT: Praeger.

Moore, D. R. (1990). Voice and choice in Chicago. In W. H. Clune & J. F. Witte (Eds.), *Choice and control in American education: The practice of choice, decentralization and school restructuring* (pp. 153–198). London: Falmer Press.

Moore, E. K. (1987). Child care in the public schools: Public accountability and the black child. In S. L. Kagan & E. F. Zigler (Eds.), *Early schooling: The national debate* (pp. 83–97). New Haven: Yale University Press.

National Association for the Education of Young Children. (1986). *Developmentally appropriate practice in early childhood programs serving children from birth through age 8.* Washington, DC: Author.

National Association for the Education of Young Children. (1996). *Developmentally appropriate practice in early childhood programs serving children from birth through age 8.* Revised position statement. Washington, DC: Author.

National Association for the Education of Young Children. (1998). *Accreditation criteria and procedures of the National Association for the Education of Young Children.* Washington, DC: Author.

National Association for the Education of Young Children. (1999). *NAEYC position statement on developing and implementing effective public policies to promote early childhood and school-age care program accreditation.* Washington, DC: Author.

National Association of State Boards of Education. (1988). *Right from the start.* Alexandria, VA: Author.

National Commission on Excellence in Education. (1983). *A nation at risk: The imperative for educational reform.* Washington, DC: U.S. Government Printing Office.

National Commission on Teaching and America's Future. (1996). *What matters most: Teaching for America's future.* New York: Author.

Neill, D. M. (1997). Transforming student assessment. *Phi Delta Kappan, 9,* 34–58.

Nodding, N. (1995). Teaching themes of caring. *Education Digest, 61*(3), 23–25.

Olson, L. (1998, February 11). The push for accountability gathers steam. *Education Week on the Web* [On-line]. Available: www.edweek.org/ew/

O'Neil, J. (2000). Fads and fireflies: The difficulties of sustaining change. *Educational Leadership, 4,* 6–9.

Osguthorpe, R. T., Harris, R. C., Harris, M. F., & Black, S. (Eds.). (1995). *Partner schools: Centers for educational renewal.* San Francisco: Jossey-Bass.

Paley, V. G. (1981). *Wally's stories.* Cambridge, MA: Harvard University Press.

Panel on Educational Technology. (1997). *Report to the president on the use of technology to strengthen K–12 education in the United States.* Washington, DC: President's Committee of Advisors on Science and Technology.

Paris, P. (1998, November). *Be different! Achieve accreditation through the uniqueness of a program.* Paper presented at the annual conference of the National Association for the Education of Young Children, Toronto, Canada.

Piaget, J. (1976). *The psychology of intelligence.* Totowa, NJ: Littlefield, Adams.

Piaget, J. (1985). *The equilibration of cognitive structures.* Chicago: University of Chicago Press.

Quality Counts. (2001). A better balance: Standards, tests, and the tools to succeed. *Education Week, 20*(17) [special issue].

Ravid, R., & Handler, M. G. (2001). *The many faces of school–university collaboration: Characteristics of successful partnerships.* Englewood, CO: Teachers Ideas Press.

Reyni, J. (1998). Building learning into the teaching job. *Educational Leadership, 55*(5), 70–74.

Reynolds, A., Temple, J., Robertson, D., & Mann, E. (2001). Long-term effects of an early childhood intervention on educational achievement and juvenile arrest: A 15-year follow-up of low-income children in public schools. *Journal of the American Medical Association, 284*(18), 2339–2346.

Rogoff, B. (1990). *Apprenticeship in thinking.* New York: Oxford University Press.

Rogoff, B. (1998). Cognition as a collaborative process. In W. Damon (Series Ed.) & R. M. Lerner (Vol. Ed.), *Handbook of child psychology: Vol. 2. Theoretical models of human development* (5th ed., pp. 679–744). New York: Wiley.

Sadovnik, A. R., & Semel, S. F. (2001). Urban school improvement: A challenge to simplistic solutions to educational problems. *Educational Researcher, 30*(9), 27–31.

Sandholtz, J. H., Ringstaff, C., & Dwyer, D. C. (1997). *Teaching with technology: Creating student-centered classrooms.* New York: Teachers College Press.

Schaps, E., Battistich, V., Solomon, D., & Watson, M. (1997). Caring school communities. *Educational Psychologist, 32,* 137–151.

Schaps, E., & Lewis, C. (1999). Perils on an essential journey: Building school community. *Phi Delta Kappan, 11,* 215–218.

Schofield, J. W. (1995). *Computers and classroom culture.* Cambridge, England: Cambridge University Press.

Shahmoon-Shanok, R. (1991). The supervisory relationship: Integrator, resource and guide. *Zero to Three, 12*(2), 16–19.

Siegel, J. (1995). The state of teacher training. *Electronic Learning, 14,* 44–48.

Sirotnik, K. A., & Goodlad, J. I. (Eds.). (1988). *School–university partnerships in action: Concepts, cases, and concerns.* New York: Teachers College Press.

Smith, L. A. (1999, November). *The positive impact that NAEYC accreditation can have on professional development, center quality and revenues, and advocacy for young children.* Paper presented at the annual conference of the National Association for the Education of Young Children, New Orleans, LA.

Sparks, D. (2000). Partnerships need purpose. *Journal of Staff Development, 21*(2), 3.

Sparks, D., & Hirsh, S. (2000, May 24). Strengthening professional development: A national strategy. *Education Week, 19*(37), 42, 45.

Stiggins, R. (2002). Assessment crisis: The absence of assessment for learning. *Phi Delta Kappan, 83*(10), 758–765.

Stott, F., & Bowman, B. T. (1996). Child development knowledge: A slippery base for practice. *Early Childhood Research Quarterly, 11,* 169–183.

Stremmel, A. (1997). Diversity and multicultural perspective. In C. Hart, D. Burts, & R. Charlesworth (Eds.), *Integrated curriculum and developmentally appropriate practice, birth to age eight* (pp. 363–388). Albany: State University of New York Press.

Technology Counts. (1999, September 23). Building the digital curriculum. *Education Week,* pp. 13–22.

Technology Counts. (2001, May 10). The new divides. *Education Week* [special issue].

Technology Counts. (2002, May 9). E-defining education. *Education Week* [special issue].

Tharp, R. G., & Gallimore, R. (1995). *Rousing minds to life: Teaching, learning, and schooling in social context.* New York: Cambridge University Press.

Trubowitz, S., & Longo, P. (1997). *How it works: Inside a school–college collaboration.* New York: Teachers College Press.

Tyack, D., & Cuban, L. (1995). *Thinking toward utopia: A century of public school reform.* Cambridge, MA: Harvard University Press.

Vaughn, M. (1998). Test scores show steady improvement. *Chicago Education, 3*(12), 1, 5.

Vygotsky, L. S. (1978). *Mind in society: The development of higher psychological processes.* Cambridge, MA: Harvard University Press.

Vygotsky, L. S. (1986). *Thought and language.* Cambridge, MA: MIT Press.

Weaver, C. (Ed.). (1998). *Reconsidering a balanced approach to reading.* Urbana, IL: National Council of Teachers of English.

Whitebook, M., Sakai, L., & Howes, C. (1997). *NAEYC accreditation as a strategy for improving child care quality.* Washington, DC: National Center for the Early Childhood Work Force.

Wiggins, G. (1998). *Educative assessment: Designing assessment to inform and improve student performance.* San Francisco: Jossey-Bass.

Zetlin, A. G., & MacLeod, E. (1995). A school–university partnership working toward the restructure of an urban school and community. *Education and Urban Society, 27*(4), 411–420.

About the Authors

JIE-QI CHEN is an associate professor of child development and early education at Erikson Institute. At Erikson, she was a co-director of the Schools Project and currently directs a project on computer technology in early education, and she co-directs another project on performance-based assessment. She is also currently a Fulbright senior specialist. Dr. Chen received a B.A. in education from Beijing Normal University in China and a Ph.D. in child development from Tufts University. She worked as a researcher at Harvard University's Project Zero, and her current research interests are the development of diverse cognitive abilities in young children; linking assessment to curriculum and instruction; the use of computer technology in early childhood classrooms; and cultural variation in child development. Dr. Chen is a coauthor of *Building on Children's Strengths: The Experience of Project Spectrum*, an editor of *Project Spectrum: Early Learning Activities*, and a contributor to the entry on multiple intelligences in *The Encyclopedia of Education*, 2nd edition.

PATRICIA HORSCH is an adjunct professor of education at Erikson Institute, where she served as a co-director of the Schools Project for the entire 11-year course of the initiative. Currently at Erikson she directs a primary school partnership between the institute and the Chicago Public Schools. She is also an independent educational consultant to public and private elementary schools. Dr. Horsch previously served as the director of the New Teacher Network at the Center for School Improvement at the University of Chicago, supporting beginning teachers in urban elementary schools through mentoring, coaching, and peer discussion and reflection groups. She was also the director of a cooperative nursery school in Chicago. Dr. Horsch received a B.A. in history from the University of North Carolina at Chapel Hill and a Ph.D. in child development from Loyola University Chicago. The topic of her dissertation, the establishment of caring learning communities in urban schools, continues to be her primary research interest.

KAREN DEMOSS is an assistant professor in the educational leadership program at the University of New Mexico. She received her B.A. in English from Austin College, her M.A. in English from Texas A&M University, and her Ph.D. in administrative, institutional, and policy studies from the University of Chicago. In 2002, her dissertation, *Political Dispositions and Education Finance Equity: An Analysis of Court Decisions Across the United States*, won the Division L Dissertation Award of the American Educational Research Association for outstanding dissertation in the area of policy and politics. While at the University of Chicago, she was a researcher for the Consortium on Chicago School Research. In her current research, Dr. DeMoss examines the ways that policy and politics influence the provision of quality education for all children. Prior to pursuing her Ph.D., Dr. DeMoss worked with a National Diffusion Network program for teacher professional development. She also served in the Peace Corps as a teacher educator, developing culturally appropriate methodologies for Mali's ministry of education, and she was the assistant director of Texas A&M's branch campus in Koriyama, Japan.

SUZANNE L. WAGNER is currently a research associate at Project Match, a Chicago-based organization that conducts program development and research activities in the fields of welfare-to-work and workforce development. Ms. Wagner also regularly collaborates on education-related projects at Erikson Institute. Current research projects in which she is involved include a multistate study of the effects of the Pathways Case Management System on both welfare agency operations and welfare recipient outcomes (a joint study by Project Match and Mathematica Policy Research) and a study of community-based employment programs in Chicago. Prior to her work at Project Match and Erikson Institute, Ms. Wagner was editor of publications at Manpower Demonstration Research Corporation (MDRC) in New York City, a nonpartisan social policy research organization. She received her B.A. from Northwestern University in English and Russian language and literature and her M.A. from the University of Michigan, Ann Arbor, in comparative literature.

RUANDA GARTH MCCULLOUGH is an assistant professor at the school of education at Loyola University Chicago. She is also a founding partner of SUCCEED Consulting, a Chicago-based firm that conducts education research, including the evaluation of the Ravinia Festival's music and jazz education programs in the Chicago Public Schools. Dr. McCullough received a B.A. in psychology and African-American studies from Wesleyan University in Middletown, Connecticut, and an M.A. and Ph.D. in urban education from the University of Chicago. While a student at the University of Chicago, she worked as a researcher for the Consortium on Chicago School Research. She was also a consultant to the Chicago Public Schools for the development and implementation of the Service Learning project. Her main areas of interest include the sociocultural foundations of education, the sociology of education, classroom processes, literacy, and school reform.

Index